CHICKPEAS

TAXI

B

D0276537

1802569252

Miss Masala.

MALLIKA BASU

BRISTOL CITY COUNCIL	
1802569252	
Bertrams	27/04/2010
641.5954	£14.99
BSSE	

Miss Masala

Real Indian cooking for busy living

MALLIKA BASU

BSSE

H
12

*** TRANSIT SLIP ***
*** DISCHARGE ON
ARRIVAL ***

Author: Basu, Mallika.
Title: Miss Masala : real
Indian cooking for busy
living
Item ID: 1802569252
Transit to: BSSE

This book is dedicated to the boss
who said I couldn't write.

First published in 2010 by Collins

HarperCollins Publishers
77-85 Fulham Palace Road,
London, W6 8JB

www.harpercollins.co.uk

Text © Mallika Basu, 2010
Illustrations © Kathryn Milton, 2010
Photographs © Neil Mersh, 2010

13 12 11 10
6 5 4 3 2 1

Mallika Basu asserts her moral right to be identified as the author
of this work. All rights reserved. No parts of this publication may be
reproduced, stored in a retrieval system or transmitted, in any form
or by any means, electronic, mechanical, photocopying, recording
or otherwise, without the prior permission of the publishers.
A catalogue record for this book is available from the British Library.

ISBN   978-0-00-730612-1

Editorial Director: Jenny Heller
Project Editor: Ione Walder
Copy Editor: Kate Parker
Design: Steve Boggs and Myfanwy Vernon-Hunt
Photography: Neil Mersh
Food: Joy Skipper
Prop Styling: Emma Thomas

Colour reproduction by
Colourscan, Singapore
Printed and bound in China

Miss Masala

Real Indian cooking for busy living

MALLIKA BASU

HY
12/11
(

Collins

This book is dedicated to the boss
who said I couldn't write.

First published in 2010 by Collins

HarperCollins Publishers
77-85 Fulham Palace Road,
London, W6 8JB

www.harpercollins.co.uk

Text © Mallika Basu, 2010
Illustrations © Kathryn Milton, 2010
Photographs © Neil Mersh, 2010

13 12 11 10
6 5 4 3 2 1

Mallika Basu asserts her moral right to be identified as the author
of this work. All rights reserved. No parts of this publication may be
reproduced, stored in a retrieval system or transmitted, in any form
or by any means, electronic, mechanical, photocopying, recording
or otherwise, without the prior permission of the publishers.
A catalogue record for this book is available from the British Library.

ISBN   978-0-00-730612-1

Editorial Director: Jenny Heller
Project Editor: Ione Walder
Copy Editor: Kate Parker
Design: Steve Boggs and Myfanwy Vernon-Hunt
Photography: Neil Mersh
Food: Joy Skipper
Prop Styling: Emma Thomas

Colour reproduction by
Colourscan, Singapore
Printed and bound in China

CONTENTS

INTRODUCTION

Squashed on a train unfit for cattle transport, in an Austin Reed suit and Kurt Geiger heels, I can think about only one thing. Rotis. Round, soft, fluffy rotis.

This is my life: 30-something girl about town, corporate superbitch and keen Indian cook. Ten years ago, just the thought of combining the three would have thrown me into a blind panic, and had me reaching for the nearest chicken tikka sandwich pack.

You see, growing up in India, I cared more about eating food than cooking it. Tantalising meals were assembled at home (although not by me) with little oil, fresh ingredients and lots of imagination, all served with limes, coriander, pickle and green finger chillies. From sweet coconut prawn curry and juicy tandoori chicken to buttery Tadka Dal and spicy-sour aloo. It was all accompanied by puffed rotis rolled and tawa-baked by our masterly cook, Dada. Oblivious to his talent, we two bespectacled sisters ate them hot, dripping with the butter we wore so proudly as lip-gloss at the dining table.

Dada was on an everyday mission – to keep it simple but delicious. As in most other Indian homes, aromatic pulaos, rich curries and deep-fried goodies were strictly reserved for weekends and special occasions. Then, Dada would turn sous-chef to my father and his elaborate kitchen feats. A keen and superb cook, my chain-smoking dad's speciality was the rice delicacy biryani. It always arrived late from a battle-ravaged kitchen.

Mother, unlike my many aunties, stayed well away from the hotbed of fiery tempers and masalas that was our Kolkata kitchen. Dabbling with the occasional spaghetti Bolognese in her psychedelic kaftan, she preferred directing and overseeing Dada's glorious Indian meals rather than troubling her good self by actually cooking them.

When I decided to leave it all behind for university in England, nobody thought to disrupt my hectic schedule of debates and rooftop parties with lessons in cooking Aloo Gobi. I arrived in rainy Buckingham, and plunged headlong into an undergraduate degree in business studies and an education in how not to eat. My experiments in the kitchen were short-lived. The burnt frozen pizzas. The tins that exploded in the microwave. The boil-in-the-bag rice that never quite cooked.

I didn't give a damn. The 90s clubbing scene was exploding around me. My love life and my finances were imploding. Homemade chicken curry was hardly going to see me through it all. Besides, I was about to embark on a master's degree in journalism. The future would be all about sharp suits, dictaphones, black cabs and mojitos. A far cry from the hair-in-bun, handloom-cotton image I had of aunties and seasoned cooks back home.

But after years of Taj Mahal takeaways and petrol station cuisine, I started aching for some good home-cooked food. I had no idea where to start, however. I needed help.

So I asked someone who had all the answers. Mother. She sent me a copy of the *National Indian Association of Women Cookbook*, given to newly wedded daughters, the soon-to-live-abroad and other hapless beings.

Armed with this seminal tome, I was ready to become Miss Masala. So what if I now worked long hours in London, spent evenings sampling cheap wine and didn't know the first thing about cooking Indian food? It couldn't be that difficult, right?

Wrong.

You see, professional Indian cooks can be a canny lot. Always happy to give you a quick breakdown of ingredients, they withhold some of the crucial basics. Perhaps as payback for all their hard graft as beginners. Aunties, on the other hand, are only too happy to oblige with recipes. But years of experience mean they use *andaaz*, giving little idea of quantities. Directions like 'Cook the onions, add some turmeric and fry with a bit of garam masala' are no good to a novice. We need specifics.

Most Indian cookbooks are no place for beginners, either. They assume the sort of basic knowledge I simply didn't have, or expect a little too much in the way of free time. Instructions like 'Soak overnight and then simmer for 3 hours' scared me half to death.

Then you have the ingredients to contend with. Indian cooking uses a seemingly endless array of specialist spices, and the magic each one brings to a dish is a mystery of Bollywood-epic proportions. Like the foul-smelling asafoetida – a deeply offensive powder but which, once cooked, infuses dishes with a magical buttery flavour.

And finally there are all those secrets you can learn only from experience. No one ever tells you, for instance, that ready-made channa masala powder plus frying onions equals three days of spicy sofa. Or that fresh curry and methi (fenugreek) leaves can be frozen for months and still retain their flavour.

Altogether it's a quagmire for the uninitiated. Thankfully, I craved the food enough to wade through it all. It was my labour of love – aided by the NIAW Cookbook, numerous international phone calls and Smirnoff vodka.

I started cooking for anyone who dared to sample it – whether keen colleague, hesitant sister or bewildered boyfriend. Low-oil and high-nutrient recipes from back home provided early inspiration, with a vindaloo or two thrown in for good measure. I was on the quest for mouth-watering dishes that I could rustle up after numbingly long days and harrowing weeks at work.

Along the way, I got married and dived into a public relations career. The art of frying onions to the perfect shade of gold now had to be combined with the science of juggling client deadlines with a hungry husband, lavish Indian functions and late-night partying. Time officially became money. Shortcuts de rigueur.

I have learnt lots of valuable lessons. That cooking when drunk is not a good idea, for instance. Especially when it's your boss who is waiting to be fed. That I would rather eat my shoe than make a samosa from scratch. And that making round, fluffy rotis plays havoc with manicured fingernails.

Most importantly, I have learnt that authentic Indian cooking is, in fact, blindingly easy and can be a regular part of frantic lives. To make gloriously aromatic pulao and creamy korma, all you need are simple recipes and basic know-how. Once you crack the essentials, the rest is a piece of chappati.

This book is all about those invaluable lessons, transferred from my kitchen to yours. It's about loving Indian food and cooking it from scratch while enjoying too many cocktails, after a steamy commute and faced with an empty fridge. The pages that follow are packed with simple recipes and handy tips for busy people who live full lives.

On some occasions an easy masala dinner will usually do the trick. But there are other nights when only a rich curry, served with heaps of basmati rice and lashings of dal and raita, will hit the spot. This book caters for such moments, whatever your mood, taste or time constraints. There are recipes for when time is of the essence, others that are big-crowd pleasers and ones for your own indulgence.

You, too, can keep it simple with quick Chicken Jhalfrezi on a bed of peppery salad leaves. Impress colleagues with a three-course dal, curry and sabzi combo. Hang out with friends, a few bottles of wine and heaps of melt-in-the-mouth lamb kebabs. And recover from it all with comforting rice Khichdi, aubergine raita and delicious little coconut bites.

Slip on your heels, keep a pair of old pyjamas handy and open your mind.

This is real Indian cooking for busy living!

Before You Start - Read This

Are you feeling somewhat inspired? Ready to take on the challenge of Indian home cooking? Have you dusted off the oversize aluminium stockpot, normally reserved for deadly punches, to make your own ghee? Invested in an industrial pestle and mortar? Convinced yourself that fermenting and sun-drying your own lime pickle is time truly well spent?

Shame.

This cookbook isn't into that sort of thing. I want to cook traditional Indian food *and* have a life. So, in a step change from time-honoured Indian cooking tradition, I blatantly advocate the use of store-bought ingredients, dinky gadgets and shortcuts. If you are a tad busy or lazy, this book is just the thing for you.

The first chapter introduces the very basics and other useful information. Tips and tricks are littered throughout the rest of the book, amongst my stories and introductions to the recipes. To avoid boring you stiff by repeating myself in the recipe descriptions, I've collected a handful of cooking tips here. Please do read these before you begin.

SOURCING INGREDIENTS

Indian spices can be bought in supermarkets, at ethnic shops or online. You could even sweet-talk your local corner shop into stocking a wide selection. And once you've bought them, you can put them to use in many different dishes, from all sorts of cuisines. If you don't have one or two of the spices specified in a dish, leave them out rather than use a substitute. Omitting a couple of the ingredients isn't going to dramatically alter the flavour of a dish. Just make sure you have the main ingredients that feature in the title or subtitle of a recipe.

A FEW WORDS ON SOME COMMONLY USED INGREDIENTS AND EQUIPMENT:

LENTILS The different types called for in Indian cooking are many and various but not really interchangeable. For more on the different varieties, see the box on page 30.

CARDAMOMS Green cardamoms are most commonly used in the recipes in this book. Occasionally brown cardamoms (also known as black cardamoms) are called for. These can't be used instead of green cardamoms, however, as they have a completely different, smoky taste.

PANEER This Indian cheese is used in a number of the recipes. It's widely available in the hard cheese section of supermarkets. You could, at a pinch, substitute it with low-fat halloumi.

CURRY LEAVES Buy these herbs in an ethnic store or the ethnic section of your local supermarket. You can use them fresh or keep a bag in the freezer and cook straight from frozen. Never use the dried leaves; they're just not the same.

GREEN FINGER CHILLIES These have a very particular flavour and can't be substituted with any other type of green chilli. If you have a problem sourcing them, buy a jar of ready-minced green chillies to keep for emergencies.

CHILLI POWDER AND WHOLE CHILLIES While on the subject on chillies, I always use extra-hot chilli powder. The milder stuff doesn't seem worth the effort, frankly. I don't deseed chillies, either. Why, when the seeds are packed with serious punch? I'm not a great fan of super-spicy food, so my recipes are on the milder side, unless otherwise stated. If you can handle it, go crazy with chillies. For more on the different types of chillies used in Indian cooking, see the box on pages 178–9. Note: bell peppers are deseeded.

YOGHURT This features extensively in Indian curries, often used to thicken curries or as a creamy, but lower fat alternative to cream. Low-fat yoghurt used straight out of the fridge will almost inevitably curdle when it touches hot oil. Use Greek yoghurt instead, which has a higher fat content, and leave it on the worktop to get it closer to room temperature before cooking. This will save your curry.

FAN-ASSISTED OVENS

Most Indian food is cooked on the hob. Where I cook a dish in the oven, I've put the temperature in Centigrade/Fahrenheit and for gas. If you have a fan-assisted electric oven, please deduct approximately 20°C (70°F) from the temperature given in the recipe and cook for the same length of time. In any case, it's always worth checking the food is cooked before you serve it.

MEASURING WITH MUGS

Everyone has a mug or cup set aside to measure rice. I use a great big builder's mug, which gives me 350g (12oz) rice – four generous portions. When I'm cooking rice or lentils, I state the amount of water needed in the form of a ratio of water to rice/lentils, e.g. 'one-and-a-half times as much water as rice' or 'twice as much water as lentils'. By using the same mug/cup, you have an easy and accurate way of adding just the right volume of water. Always check the rice with a fork at the end of cooking. Depending on its quality, you may sometimes need to add an extra half a cup of hot water to get it cooked just right.

ESSENTIAL GADGETS

Pestles and mortars are wonderful. But I'm not keen on bits of garlic, ginger and whole spices flying into my hair, face and clothes. A cheap mini electric coffee grinder works wonders to powder roasted spices. A hand blender can purée ingredients in seconds, without taking up much shelf space in the kitchen. See the box on page 49 on how to make your own ginger and garlic pastes.

COOKING OILS

You'll see that I generally don't specify a particular type of cooking oil. You can use any type of neutral flavour oil (sunflower, vegetable, groundnut, etc.), just not olive oil. For more on this, see the box on page 54.

PRECOOKING VEGETABLES

Try not to parboil or shallow-fry vegetables before cooking them. It is too much extra effort and you lose their essential nutrients. Also, the longer veggies get with the spices, the better they will taste.

COOKING ON A HIGH HEAT

I tend to cook over a high heat on the hob, so that the ingredients cook more quickly. But do reduce the heat slightly if a pot is boiling too vigorously or fried ingredients are browning too quickly and in danger of burning.

A WORD ON SALT

I consume far too much salt. Which, I've been led to believe, will cause me untold grief in the form of hideous illnesses before I turn 40. I'll spare you a similar fate by leaving salt addition in my recipes to your own discretion. The best thing to do is add a little at a time right at the end of a recipe until you get it to taste just the way you like it.

INDIAN COOKING TERMS

To help with the strange Indian words that pepper these pages, just turn to the glossary at the back of this book.

AND LASTLY

Please don't worry if your chicken curry doesn't match the exact shade of sienna orange in the fancy photograph. The hue of your home-cooked feast will depend on the brand of spices, type of ingredients and the lighting in your kitchen. As always, it's the taste that counts.

Now for the rest. Happy cooking!

1.

FROM BHUNA TO BALTI

Getting to know Indian food and the very basics

Miss Masala.

ACHIEVING 'AUNTYDOM' WAS NEVER GOING TO BE EASY.

Such high standards. So many spices, so little time. No information on what they actually do. Or how best to use them, for that matter. I started my quest with a trip to the nearest aunty, conveniently located in Birmingham – epicentre of the British curry phenomenon.

The door flew open and Aunty launched into high-pitched squawks about how thin I looked. In my family, being thin is considered an even worse fate than left-handedness, singledom or unemployment. More cries of 'gaunt/tired/malnourished' were the cue for me to step into the kitchen where Aunty, a senior Indian Diplomatic Officer, had laid out a dazzling four-piece, home-cooked meal.

Aunty lamented the sorry state of the Indian government, the rise of the balti and the problem with young people today. I worked my way through the coconut and raisin dal, chilli pumpkin stir-fry and spicy chicken curry, agreeing and wondering what possessed me to aspire to such dizzying culinary heights.

If Aunty was to be believed, everything was 'so easy to make'. The dishes, authentic recipes passed down from her great-great-grandmother's north Kolkata kitchen, took 'no time at all'. My hopes were fading fast, like the empty space in my rapidly filling stomach.

But I dared not mention this to her. The size-eight-one-who-was-wasting-away would need to be comatose or sick before she was allowed to stop eating. I contemplated faking a fainting spell as she heaped more basmati rice on to my plate.

The next day, we visited a local curry house. Inspired by the delights of the previous night's authentic Indian meal, I took a fresh, critical look at the fare that had, until now, been my happy respite from three-for-a-fiver microwave meals. I reflected on several interesting things:

1. The word 'curry' means 'sauce' or 'gravy' in India. In the UK, on the other hand, it's used as a generic term for pretty much all Indian, Pakistani and Bangladeshi food. Not all our dishes are curries – there are bharta, bhuna, tandoori and kadai dishes, and many others besides. In a nod to popular British culture, however, I have used the words 'curry' and 'Indian food' interchangeably throughout this book.

But don't get me on to balti, which means 'bucket'. Fancy dinner out of a bucket? Me neither. Some say balti originated from the Kashmiri province of Baltistan. The truth is that the word was coined by a clever Brummie and has as little to do with cooking as my ceramic hair irons.

2. This creativity extends to restaurant menus. Many of the popular British curry dishes don't exist in India. Such as phal (mouth-numbingly hot), madras (fluorescent red and gloopy), and chicken tikka masala (no description needed). The perfect greasy end to an alcohol-ridden evening they *are*. Indian they are *not*.

Interestingly, chicken tikka masala has had the rare privilege of infiltrating many restaurant menus in India. It is based on a far more delectable, decadent and diet-defying dish, Murgh Makhani (also known as 'butter chicken'), which is sadly harder to find in the UK.

3. The range of dishes at a standard local curry house is pretty limited. The same cubes of pre-prepared meat are stirred into a set number of curries, depending on what you fancy. Where are the sweet, light Bengali curries? The coconut-filled south Indian dishes? The rich, spicy feasts from Mughal-inspired Hyderabad and Lucknow? And the famous fusion cuisine of the Parsis and Goans? Even the few recognisably Indian dishes on the menu are transformed beyond recognition before they arrive at the table.

MY MOST HATED UK CURRY LINGO

Naan bread
Naan is bread, so this translates as 'bread bread'. Plain wrong.
Pulao rice
'Pulao' means 'flavoured rice'. I rest my case.
Poppadom
In Hindi, this is 'papad', which is conveniently shorter.

IT WAS TIME FOR ME TO SACRIFICE MY LOVE of the local takeaway on the altar of authentic Indian home cooking. Aunty sent me off with a 20-piece dinner set from the local cash and carry. I returned to my ex-council apartment and promptly made my way to the inventively named 'Indian Spice Shop' in Euston.

The Indian Spice Shop was as much a part of my teenage years as George Michael and Clearasil. Our family summer holidays in Europe always ended with a few weeks in London, by which time the words *schnitzel*, *strudel* and *steak frites* sent a chill down my spine. I happily played bag carrier to Mother as she stocked up on masalas, pickle and ready-made chappatis for our short-let central London apartment.

But I was alone now. I went round this monument to the art of sub-continental cooking with a rusty basket. Shelves were stacked high with spices, flour, basmati rice, pickles and lentils. I had a list, but it seemed pointless. Where do I start? Where is Mother when I need her?

The owner came to my rescue. To this guy, a first-time masala buyer sticks out like an unaccompanied man in the M&S lingerie department. He advised me to buy the smallest quantities, as you always use less than you think and the flavour of the spices quickly fades.

With that tiny titbit, I started building my collection. The dried spices needed for Indian cooking come in two types – whole and powdered – and are known as masalas. The same word applies to a mix of spices. And it can, confusingly, also refer to a paste of dried spices with fresh ingredients, such as onions, garlic and ginger. First I bought the very basics – the ingredients used in many of the recipes I had bookmarked to try.

WHOLE SPICES

SIZZLED IN HOT OIL AT THE BEGINNING OF
COOKING TO RELEASE SUBTLE AROMAS

Bay leaves (TEJ PATTA) – Woody leaves of the laurel plant.
Black peppercorns (KALI MIRCH) – Pungent whole peppercorns.
Cloves (LAVANG) – Strong and minty flower buds.
Green cardamoms (ELAICHI) – Fragrant seedpods.
Cinnamon (DALCHINI) sticks – Sharp and sweet bark of a tree.
Cumin (JEERA) – Warm and earthy seeds.
Red chillies (LAL MIRCH) – Long fiery red chillies.

 # POWDERED SPICES

ADDED LATER TO INJECT THE DISH WITH INTENSE FLAVOURS

Coriander (DHANIYA) – Warm and lemony powdered seeds.
Cumin (JEERA) – Earthy powdered seeds.
Turmeric (HALDI) – Bitter and luminous-yellow powdered root.
Chilli (LAL MIRCH) – Powdered fiery chillies.
Garam masala – A blend of the whole spices (see above),
roasted and powdered.

The initial stash was going to keep me going for some time,
according to Masala Man. So next I stocked up on the fresh
ingredients, used in between adding the whole and powdered spices.
These perishable ingredients would clearly need to be purchased
more frequently, at my local supermarket for convenience.

FRESH INGREDIENTS
Root ginger / Garlic / Green finger chillies
Bunch of coriander leaves / Bag of curry leaves
Onions / Greek yoghurt

MISS MASALA HAD ARRIVED. And Keema Mattar was my first recipe of choice. Highly satisfying with some pitta bread, this also appealed because it needed no more skill than a deft hand to jab mince with a wooden spoon. The long list of ingredients had all been duly acquired.

Gripped with feverish excitement, I set the oil to heat and quickly chucked in the whole spices. Next, I threw in the onions, ginger and garlic and stirred gently, waiting for them to brown. They didn't for ages. So I lost patience and added everything else. The result was a crunchy onion and mince concoction that was as far away from India as I was from opening my own restaurant.

I had followed every instruction (almost) to the letter. So I couldn't have been very far from the real thing. Down but not out, I tried the recipe again the following week. And this time, it came out just the way I remembered from our weekday dinners at home.

It seemed that the most basic ingredient for Indian cooking was patience. Creating the perfect kebab was never going to be as straightforward as opening a bag of ready-prepared salad. Or as quick. In fact, the word 'quick', when applied to Indian cooking, is truly relative. Considering some recipes take up to a day of soaking, chopping and stirring, half an hour to make a mixed vegetable curry is essentially fast food.

The secret of cooking the food just right lies in timing. Indian cookbooks are full of vague instructions like 'when the onions are cooked' or 'when the masalas are ready'. Knowing when the moment is right is essential, because ingredients are added in stages. A group of spices is added only when the previous lot has changed hue, aroma or texture. But I had to work out for myself when the dish was ready for the next addition, because no one ever explains it.

I learnt with the keema that I should have waited until the oil was hot before starting to cook. Next, added any whole spices like cloves, cinnamon and bay leaves. As they started sizzling, I should have tossed in the chopped onions and fried them until golden brown. It was my job to watch the lot. Which sounds exhausting, but actually is easy to get the hang of. After a few goes, I was on autopilot.

Keema Mattar
Minced meat with peas and fresh coriander

My favourite Pakistani restaurant has the dubious strap line 'probably the best tandoori restaurant in London'. I once asked the waiter about the ingredients in their Keema Mattar. Beef mince, he replied, helpfully.

Beef isn't eaten by Hindus in India. Only the really bad ones like me. After years of blood, sweat and tears (I do like a bit of drama), I finally came up with a recipe that uses more than just mince and less than a page of ingredients. It's as simple to make as spaghetti Bolognese and chilli con carne but a happy respite from both. You could just as easily use lamb mince for this moist but curry-free dish.

Feeds 4

1 large onion
2.5cm (1in) root ginger
2 garlic cloves
1 tbsp oil
whole spices
  2 bay leaves
  8 cloves
  8 cardamoms
  5cm (2in) cinnamon stick
  10 whole black peppercorns
1 tsp coriander powder
1 tsp cumin powder
½ tsp turmeric powder
½ tsp chilli powder
4 tbsp tomato purée
2 fresh green finger chillies
4 tbsp natural Greek yoghurt
500g (1lb 2oz) lean minced beef or lamb
1 mug of frozen peas
½ tsp garam masala
25g (1oz) fresh coriander, roughly chopped
salt

1. Peel and finely chop the onion, ginger and garlic. Pour the oil into a medium pan set over a high heat. When the oil is hot, add the whole spices. Within seconds they will start spluttering, and you'll be able to smell their heady aromas.

2. Now add the onion and fry for 5 minutes until it starts to go a pale gold. Stir in the ginger and garlic, and fry for a further 5 minutes until the masala mixture caramelises, turning a golden brown.

3. Next add all the powdered spices bar the garam masala. Fry them for about 5 minutes, stirring constantly with a wooden spoon. If the spices get stuck to the bottom of the pan, add a tablespoon of hot water to release them while stirring and scraping the base of the pan with the spoon.

4. Then stir in the tomato purée and fry for a further minute. Lower the heat and simmer for 5–10 minutes until you can see the oil beginning to rise to the surface of the mixture. Meanwhile, roughly chop the green finger chillies. »

5. Turn the heat up high once again, and add the yoghurt, chillies and mince. Stir like a maniac so that the meat browns evenly and there are no large lumps in it. Then add half a mug of hot water and leave to simmer, uncovered, for 15 minutes.

6. Finally, add the peas and simmer for about 5 minutes until they're cooked. Add salt to taste, and stir in the garam masala and chopped coriander to finish.

7. Keema is divine served with toasted pitta bread or hot rotis, along with some mango pickle and a dollop of creamy, natural Greek yoghurt.

WITH ALL INDIAN RECIPES THERE ARE SOME OBVIOUS SIGNS FOR WHEN TO MOVE ON TO THE NEXT STAGE OF COOKING:

>> The oil is sufficiently hot if it forms little bubbles when you touch it with your wooden spoon.
>> Whole spices are ready when they sizzle and release pungent aromas.
>> Dried spices, whole and powdered, each have their own strong smell, which will tone down when cooked.
>> Onions are cooked when they are evenly golden brown but not burnt.
>> Tomatoes are cooked when they disintegrate.
>> A combination of dried spices and other ingredients is ready when, having been cooked on a slow simmer, oil starts oozing out of little holes in the mixture.
>> Lentils are done when they lose their shape and become integrated with the cooking water to form a thick soup.

AN IMPORTANT TRICK, I LEARNT, is to whack the heat up high and stir like a maniac to prevent the spices from getting stuck to the bottom of the pan and burning. As I explained to my uninitiated sister: don't make love to it, fuck it! If the spices do get stuck on the bottom of the pan, just add a couple of tablespoons of hot water from the kettle and scrape them off.

Initially this meant giving each pan of food my undivided attention, a boring task that is broadly comparable to watching cheap nail colour dry. It's not difficult, but until you get the hang of it you have to pay attention and avoid getting distracted. With this revelation I embraced my next Indian cooking attempt – the Mattar Paneer. The stakes were getting higher. This is a classic north Indian dish made with Indian cheese and peas. To destroy this recipe would be tantamount to committing curry hara-kiri.

True to form, I dived straight into the recipe. But midway through the frying-onions stage, extreme boredom set in. I wandered off to pour myself a glass of wine. Then fired off an impassioned e-mail to a friend on the idiocy of men. By which time, the onions had started to burn, bringing the attempt to an untimely and tragic conclusion.

Of course, there is no shame in burnt curry. As with many things in life, like perms and financial journalism, it is better to have tried and failed to cook Indian food than to have never tried at all.

Mattar Paneer
Curried Indian cheese with tomatoes and peas

Paneer is Indian cheese – a firm favourite with vegetarian Indians and yours truly. Cooked paneer has the texture of tofu and the moreishness of good-quality buffalo mozzarella. Stone cold, however, it has all the allure of cubed polystyrene.

Luckily, paneer is only served steaming hot as chunks of loveliness nestled amidst a melange of spiced ingredients. I tried making it from scratch once, with disappointing results. Buy it ready-made from the hard cheese section of your local supermarket and focus your efforts on the recipe instead.

Feeds 4

Vegetarian
1 large onion
4cm (1½in) root ginger
4 garlic cloves
3 medium tomatoes
250g (9oz) paneer
2 tbsp oil
1 tsp kasoori methi (optional)
2 tsp coriander powder
1 tsp cumin powder
½ tsp turmeric powder
½ tsp chilli powder
3 tbsp natural Greek yoghurt
1 mug of frozen peas
½ tsp garam masala
salt

1. Peel and finely chop the onion, ginger, garlic and tomatoes and cut the paneer into bite-sized pieces. The best way to do this is to first halve and then quarter the block of cheese lengthways, then cut through the width at even intervals.

2. Pour 1 tablespoon of the oil into a large frying pan set over a high heat. When the oil is hot, fry the paneer cubes until golden for 1 minute on one side and a further minute on the opposite side. This will prevent the cheese from crumbling later. Remove the pieces with a slotted spoon and set aside.

3. Leave the kasoori methi (if using) to soak in 2 tablespoons of hot water. Next pour the remaining oil into the same frying pan. When the oil is hot, stir in the onion, ginger and garlic and fry for about 10 minutes until pale golden. Now stir in all the powdered spices apart from the garam masala, add the tomatoes and fry for another 5 minutes, jabbing the masala mixture with your wooden spoon to help it disintegrate and form a thick paste. You may need to add a little hot water to prevent the mixture from sticking to the bottom of the pan. »

4. Lower the heat to a simmer, add the yoghurt and stir it in well. Now wait for the oil to ooze through little pores in the masala mixture, stirring from time to time until this happens. When it does, after about 2 minutes, mix in the peas and half a mug of hot water. Cook for another 3 minutes, then season with salt to taste and chuck in the garam masala, paneer chunks and the kasoori methi (if using) along with its water.

5. Add another half mug of hot water to cook the whole lot for 5 minutes. Once oil floats to the top, serve the Mattar Paneer hot with some warm ready-made naans and creamy natural Greek yoghurt.

INTRODUCING KASOORI METHI

Kasoori methi, dried bitter fenugreek leaves, works miracles to balance the sweetness of curried dishes. It's sold alongside other dried spices and is at its finest first soaked in a tablespoon of hot water and then added along with the liquid to the dish towards the end of cooking.

ABOVE Keema Mattar (page 21)
CENTRE Perfectly Fluffy Basmati (page 31)

ABOVE Mattar Paneer (page 24)
ABOVE RIGHT Berry Dal (page 29)

MY SECOND ATTEMPT AT MATTAR PANEER was a triumph – a
culinary phoenix that rose, quite literally, from the ashes. Bright-eyed and
optimistic, I carried on valiantly. Climbing at work to the heady heights
of PR manager and moving to a modern apartment block, albeit in grim
Elephant and Castle. And gaining enough confidence to add more spices to
my collection. Mustard seeds, dried mango powder, asafoetida and tamarind
paste made it to my bulging 'Indian' kitchen shelf. Familiar dishes from my
childhood were tried from the *NIAW Cookbook*, with mixed results.

But I felt empowered. Emboldened. Excited. I sealed my fate by having a
go at the age-old dal recipe passed down the generations of my maternal
grandmother's Berry (pronounced 'Bay-ree') family.

Berry Dal
Simple buttery lentils – a family favourite

Some of the best holidays I had as a child were in Delhi, India's capital city. Mother used to pack us off to her family home with Nani, her strong-willed mum. And we spent the days rolling around being spoilt by various uncles and aunties, nourished on a diet of Berry Dal, fresh chappatis, sabzi and homemade pickles.

This dal uses tadka (pronounced 'tur-ka') – a magical mix of spices sizzled in hot oil – to infuse the dish with flavour. I remember dal being served thick, a consistency created by adding a little hot water at a time and only when the lentils dry up and start spluttering on to the kitchen tiles.

Feeds 4

Vegetarian
125g (4½oz) huskless moong (split yellow) lentils
¼ tsp turmeric powder
1 tsp ghee
1 pinch of asafoetida
1 tsp cumin seeds
1 dried long red chilli
¼ tsp chilli powder
salt

1. Place the lentils in a sieve and rinse thoroughly under a cold tap until the water runs clear. Then put them in a medium pan and cover with twice as much cold water as lentils. Add the turmeric and boil gently on a medium heat, keeping alert for the first couple of minutes to make sure the pan doesn't boil over.

2. As it boils, the dal will produce scum, which you need to skim off the surface. Every time the lentils begin to dry out, add a little bit more hot water. The consistency of this dal should be thick, like soup from a carton.

3. When the lentils start integrating with the water in the pan, which will take about 20 minutes, you can make the tadka. Heat the ghee in a small frying pan. When it begins to bubble, add the asafoetida. This stuff smells disgusting – you have been warned – but tastes amazing! Then add the cumin seeds, the chilli pepper and the chilli powder. Let it all sizzle for a few seconds and then pour the tadka over the dal.

4. Heat the dal for another minute as you mix in the tadka. Add salt to taste, and voilà, the Berry Dal is ready. This is best eaten with rotis dunked in it.

LOVING LENTILS

Forget the horrors of boiled pulses. Dal is a piping-hot bowl of
delicately spiced lentil curry. A must with every Indian meal.
Soft and buttery, each dal has its own special cooking time and
addition of spices known as tadka (also called baghar or chaunk).

My first lentil shopping trip was totally overwhelming.
Lentils come in green, brown, yellow and red, some with husks
and others skinless. The variety is quite bewildering, as is
how to cook each type. I used my tried-and-tested, scientific
method to master cooking them: buy one small bagful and perfect
it after several failed attempts. The trick is to buy 500g
(1lb 2oz) of a variety at a time and never, ever replace
the lentils in one dal recipe for another. These are the
types of lentil typically used in Indian dishes:

MASOOR - SPLIT RED LENTILS.
Widely available and super quick to cook.
A real winner in my books.

TOOR - SPLIT YELLOW LENTILS.
Also known as Arhar or Tuvar. These are shaped like flat discs,
sometimes sold with an oil coating that you can just wash off.
Popularly used in south Indian dals.

CHANNA - A SMALLER RELATIVE OF THE CHICKPEA.
It's split in half to create a yellow lentil. It has a sweet,
nutty flavour and is often cooked with sweet vegetables or sugar.

MOONG - A GREEN PULSE THAT CAN BE SPLIT AND
DE-HUSKED TO GIVE AN OVAL-SHAPED YELLOW LENTIL.
The green stuff is a great stodgy winter choice, while
the yellow version gives a lighter perennial option.

THERE. I HAD IT. The finest homemade dal, Mattar Paneer and Keema Mattar. The three ideal basics for my first ever, complete Indian meal. All I still needed was to master the art of fluffy basmati rice.

This was easier than I thought. My father arrived in London for his annual summer holiday. I invited him over for some of my newly perfected, quick Indian home cooking. He brought along a brand new, Iranian Pars Khazar rice cooker. Handing me the large box, he declared that every girl's new home needs a rice cooker. For the first time since I was two, I agreed with him instantly.

For good measure, he also handed over his fail-safe recipe for perfect basmati rice.

Perfectly Fluffy Basmati
Steaming hot rice for every Indian meal

I never cook anything but white basmati rice when eating Indian food. I've read all about how it's lower in fat than other long-grain rice. But honestly, it's the light, fluffy texture and nutty fragrance that does it for me.

For a brief, seriously healthy spell I tried making brown basmati instead. This is packed full of fibre and even healthier that the white variety. But it takes a bit of getting used to with a curry. So I use it only to serve with other, non-Indian meals.

Feeds 4
Vegetarian
350g (12oz) basmati rice

1. Having weighed the rice in the kitchen scales, measure it out again in a mug – taking note of the number of mugfuls – and place in a medium pan. Fill the pan with cold water. With one hand, stir the rice for a minute to release the dust from the rice into the water.

2. Next drain the rice and, using the same mug, add one-and-a-half times as much hot water as rice into the same pan. By measuring the water in this way, you are adding only as much as the rice needs to absorb while cooking. No need for draining or second-guessing! »

31

3. Bring the pan to a boil, then lower the heat to a simmer, cover with a lid and cook for 10–15 minutes until the water is all absorbed and the rice is cooked through. Never stir the rice while cooking because that releases starch and makes it all gloopy. If you desperately want to prod the rice to check it, use a fork instead of a spoon. Once the rice is ready, keep the lid on the pan for 2 minutes to let the steam release any grains stuck to the bottom. Then scoop on to a plate and attack.

JALDI JALDI

 ## QUICK TRICKS FOR THE GODDESS IN YOU

Getting to grips with the recipes was one thing. Retrofitting them into my life was quite another.

In the early days, I made grand plans to further my cooking prowess. Never mind deadlines. I was going to powder my own garam masala. Marinate meat overnight. Cook raw chickpeas for hours as recommended by the latest cookery magazine. All the while, maintaining the karmic calm of a stoned Himalayan sadhu.

I soon realised that the truly inspirational cookery programme was presented by a celebrity with a crack team of experts. Invisible to the outside world, like Santa's elves, they ran around her, shopping, chopping, cleaning and washing up, while others did her hair and mopped her brow.

I, on the other hand, had no one but my meagre self and a long list of urgent priorities. Work paid the bills. Friends were essential for fun. Men were high maintenance. Painting nails and updating my wardrobe were critical. Fashioning shortcrust dough into triangular-shaped samosas was not.

I decided that spending unnecessarily long toiling in the kitchen ranked close to ironing jeans and drinking Liebfraumilch. Daily slaving over a steaming pot simply wasn't for me. The goddess in me needed shortcuts. Anything to make my life easier. This, believe it or not, was how Dada and my aunties operated too. I didn't actually know anyone who made his or her own garam masala back home.

During my next food-shopping trip, I contemplated the complex equation of effort vs. reward. The answer seemed to be a pot of curry powder. This pre-mixed ingredient is the mainstay of recipes in dog-eared women's magazines at the dentist and the doctor's. On the surface, it sounds like a godsend. A blend of essential whole spices such as cumin, coriander, chilli, cloves, black pepper, etc., ground into an all-purpose curry powder. Ready for whatever Indian dish you are planning to cook.

Easy, but so boring. I tried it with chicken. Then lamb. Next with vegetables. Everything tasted the same – of supermarket own-brand curry powder. This isn't in the spirit of true Indian cooking. Half the fun is in the variation, adding a little bit of this and a little bit of that to end up with something truly unique. It was also far too reminiscent of the dried fruit and nut British homemade curries of the 70s. I cast the stuff aside and made once more for my haven of masala salvation – the Indian Spice Shop.

Here, I sought another vaguely familiar spice shortcut of the past. In my student years, Mother had taken to sending me presents via any willing London-bound relative. The parcels contained contact-lens solution ('much cheaper in India'), boxes of sugary Indian mithai and cartons of recipe-specific spice blends, including ready-mixed meat masala, chicken masala and the optimistically named Kitchen King.

Alas, I hadn't made the most of these gifts. My student brain cells had been reserved for the pursuit of an education in business, contemporary fashion and the exploration of illegal substances. But now I was a changed person. A clean and respectable, tax-paying, law-abiding goddess-in-the-making. I loaded the rickety basket with channa masala and kadai gosht masala and filled whatever space was left with cartons of Kitchen King.

In my apartment, the back-of-the-pack recipe for sautéed chickpeas instantly appealed. I stir-fried some onions and tomatoes; added 3 tablespoons of channa masala powder, and the tinned legumes became my new best friend. I sighed, 'You complete me' under my breath as I toasted wholemeal pitta bread. And then the doorbell rang.

It was a fellow would-be goddess in pink velour track pants – my neighbour from downstairs. Also third cousin, i.e. immediate family, and close friend. She wanted to borrow some serving dishes. 'Are you cooking channa?' she enquired as I threw the door open. 'Yes. Doesn't it smell great?' I replied. I quickly ate a massive bowlful in front of the telly after she left and put away the leftovers to take for lunch at work. But as I walked through the corridor the next morning, nose twitching, I wondered what the neighbours thought of my kitchen wizardry.

It wasn't just the corridor of our porter-guarded tower block that had been overtaken by the potent whiff of the spice blend. It had infiltrated my two tiny bedrooms, the inbuilt closets, my jewellery chest and every millimetre of upholstery. I frantically aired the flat, opening windows wide and lighting scented candles, but the smell of channa masala lingered on. Three days later when my neighbour came over to return the dishes and chat, I could smell the stuff emanating through the pores of the battered blue Ikea sofa.

The first lesson here was that chickpeas are the ultimate Indian fast food. The second and more important lesson was that ready-made spice blends do not always the best shortcuts make. The search for culinary tricks continued well into the next year of my big cooking adventure. And this is what I concluded: spices smell, so plan Indian cooking carefully.

Curry hair is never going to be the height of style. Every time I rushed out to party after a spot of cooking, I might as well have been balancing a pot of saag gosht on my head. Too self-conscious to show off my dance moves, I'd stand in a corner and drink myself silly instead. My dinner-party guests were subjected to it, too. No one ever thanked me for dry-cleaning bills for coats smelling of the jeera aloo I had served earlier.

The truth is that Indian spices smell pretty strong. I couldn't avoid using them, so I just got smarter about managing them. It was a bit like smoking in my teenage years. Knowing my parents might catch me lighting up in the house didn't make me stop – just encouraged me to stock up on air freshener and chewing gum.

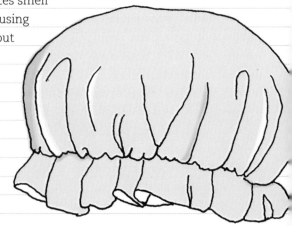

THIS IS HOW TO SET YOUR HOME FREE OF SMELLS:

COOK A DAY IN ADVANCE IF POSSIBLE.

A bit of clever social diarising and the night before a dinner party is a quiet one in. I cook all the food early and put it in the fridge to reheat the following evening. I don't worry about serving guests stale food because Indian cuisine always tastes better the next day. Ingredients slowly soak up all those heady spices and develop far more intense flavours. In India, leftovers served at an 'after' party are always better than food freshly cooked for the party itself. My guests are inadvertently bestowed a great honour and cherish me even more for it. (I'm guessing.)

When I'm being super well organised (a rare feat), I cook a few days in advance and freeze the dishes. All they need is overnight defrosting and, again, a quick reheat before the meal. With the cooking dealt with in advance, on the actual day I can spend the time tidying up, getting changed and placing flowers in vases.

DRESS APPROPRIATELY.

I'm not Eric the dry-cleaner's favourite customer for nothing. I often come home battle-worn from work or desperately hungry after a few drinks with friends and start cooking in my suit. While snacking on microwaved papads and mango pickle.

It's taken a hefty cleaning bill to partly shake off this messy habit. Now my top trick is to quickly change into a pair of old pyjamas and don a shower cap to protect my hair. The shower cap looks stupid. But it does save me the bother of washing and recreating the do when there was nothing wrong with it in the first place. And I can rip the cap off in seconds if someone shows up unexpectedly.

IF YOU'RE IN A RUSH, COOK LOW-SMELL RECIPES.

Usually, I'm dashing around on public transport. Racing to get dinner on the table before that all-important episode of a vacuous TV talent show. Or trying to line my stomach before a long night ahead. With a strictly limited window of opportunity to transform from spice girl to sizzling siren.

For occasions like this, low-smell recipes are the best ones to go for. As a rule, frying onions with lots of powdered spices will fill you and your kitchen with strong aromas. The dishes to go for are a one-pot healthy pulao or a dal brimming with vegetables. If I do choose to make a curry, I pick those that use only a few spices or have a herby base.

AND FINALLY, PREPARE THE HOME.

I'm no Mrs Beeton, but keeping an apartment smelling fresh and wonderful is pure common sense. I keep the kitchen door shut tight and the windows open wide to prevent aromas from creeping into the other rooms. Then the scented candles come out. For a bit of added authenticity, I have a stash of super-strong incense sticks at the ready. Play some Bollywood tunes and it's the perfect setting for a proper Indian meal.

Before I move on, though, I have to say this. If you don't like the aroma of Indian food, you're reading the wrong book. If it's your man who doesn't like it, this is the perfect moment to finally rid yourself of him.

Gizmos and Gadgets SAVING THOSE PRECIOUS MINUTES

Inspired by the equipment used by professional cooks, I bought sturdy aluminium pots and pans for cooking Indian food. Big mistake. Those professional types have extra-strong arm muscles and masses of patience (not to mention an army of underlings to scrape off the leftovers). They also don't get distracted by *The X Factor* and glitter-vest ironing. I discovered soon enough that the best shortcut of all is to use the highest-quality non-stick cookware I could afford.

It started a mini revolution in my kitchen. Within a week I had bought my first ever hand blender. This miraculous gadget saves nails like a Korean manicurist. I could now purée fresh ginger and garlic, whiz up some kebab marinade and even make a mango lassi. Thankfully for me, the blender came with completely idiot-proof instructions and a splatter-proof beaker.

Over the years, I have amassed a grand collection of kitchen gadgets, some exceptionally useful and others utterly pointless. The chopper does a remarkable job of dicing small quantities of vegetables like onion, cucumber, root ginger and garlic. The rice cooker I will take to my grave. The mini electric coffee grinder finely powders in seconds homemade spice blends for dhansak, sambhar and tandoori chicken.

The food processor, on the other hand, is scary to look at. Exhausting to drag from its special shelf and monstrous on the worktop. Except for grinding small quantities of dry ingredients, the mortar calls for too much pestling. The less said about the juicer and the herb chopper the better.

The most life-changing of all gadgets has, without a smidgen of doubt, been the pressure cooker. No Indian kitchen is complete without a selection of them in different sizes. I wasn't always convinced, though. My first doubts about it were sown in my friend's New York kitchen. Turns out she put some vegetables in the contraption and wandered off to shower and blow-dry her hair. The next thing she heard was a muffled explosion. If the battered pan wasn't enough to send a shudder through her Molton Browned body, there was green vegetable mush plastered all over the ceiling.

An internal voice instructed me to stay as far away from explosive kitchen devices as possible. But once I'd learnt not to get too distracted and wander off, I couldn't help warming to the idea of a pressure cooker. What's not to like? It cuts cooking time by using steam pressure on the food, saves electricity and, by default, the world. Who says a goddess can't be a part-time eco-warrior?

The first time I used one, I sat patiently at the kitchen table waiting for the reassuring whistle. Too scared to go anywhere; too petrified of what might go wrong. Nothing ever did. Now I've acquired two. One large one and a smaller version perfect for a meal for two.

TOP PRESSURE-COOKER TIPS

1. Never fill the pan to more than a third.
2. When cooking dal, wash well and add a teaspoon of oil to reduce foaming.
3. Fry up your spices first in the same pan before you stick the lid on, rather than frying them up separately and adding them after the dish is cooked, as they will still taste raw.
4. Don't shake the pan when the lid is on.
5. Release steam by gently lifting the weight on top with a long-handled wooden spoon and keep out of the way of the little vent holes.

Cooking Shortcuts THE SEARCH CONTINUES...

Alongside my quest for life-changing gadgets ran the search for food shortcuts. The attempt to make my own paneer started it. I curdled almost a gallon of milk but ended up with only a tiny block of too crumbly cheese. This was clearly the food equivalent of big box, little present. For a whole day's work too – Google research included.

It hardly encouraged me to make my own coconut milk, garam masala, ghee or tomato purée. Ready-to-use ingredients form the basis of a multi-billion-pound industry for good reason. I salute them. Particularly the ones that offer high quality and convenience. Sadly, some solutions – like ready-puréed ginger and garlic – don't always make the cut. They can be more anaemic than the real thing. I keep a store-bought jar of each handy but if you have the time, these two ingredients are definitely worth fiddling over (see the box on page 49).

MY FAVOURITE COOKING SHORTCUTS

» Freshly frozen spinach and peas.
» Frozen grated coconut (from any Oriental supermarket)
  and coconut milk.
» Tinned chickpeas, black-eyed beans and kidney beans.
» Ready-to-cook frozen parathas – both plain and
  stuffed with onion.
» Ready-made chappatis/rotis.

THE TRUTH ABOUT MAKING GHEE

I would love to make ghee from scratch some day. But I couldn't
possibly recommend it. It takes 3 hours plus to make. My entire
flat would then stink of grease for the rest of eternity. Far
better just to stick to the bought stuff.

Simplify Meals

Back home in India, meals ranged from little snack platters to multi-course madness. The elaborate ones featured dal, a meat or fish curry, two vegetable side dishes served with papads, deep-fried shredded potatoes, salad and raita. These were served at weekends and extended family dinners.

Then there were the simple Indian meals, mainly for weekdays or weekend brunches. Like a lamb pulao with Kachumbar Raita. Or shallow-fried parathas stuffed with spiced carrots and served with a selection of pickles and thick natural yoghurt.

And finally, there were the intermittent snacks. The little nibbly things for when you came home famished from swimming lessons or drama classes. Like aloo tikkis and fish chops – little pan-fried croquettes served with coriander and mint chutney.

The same principles apply in my kitchen. Except that we like variety. So Indian curries are limited to two meals a week. My trick is to keep it simple when it's just the two of us on a weekday. Choose one or two wholesome dishes and serve them up with something low fuss. For example:

>> Rice and lentil Khichdi (see page 194) and crispy papads (see below)
>> Keema, vegetable dal and piping hot basmati rice
(see page 31 for a fail-safe recipe)
>> Paneer Bhujia (see page 113) with toasted pitta bread
>> Masala Fish (see page 60) and a green leaf salad

COOKING CRISPY PAPADS

For the best results, cook for 1 minute on high in the microwave. No need for a plate. If you don't have a microwave, pop directly on the hob (gas or electric) for 1 minute, turning until evenly crispy on both sides.

Cooking two or more dishes at the same time calls for some dedication. So this I reserve for weekends when I push the boat out with a few additional dishes like raita or sabzi. This works wonders for when a friend pops in too. I might make:

>> Methi Murgh, Baingan Bharta (see pages 85–6)
   and Fluffy Basmati Rice (see page 31)
>> Chicken Jhalfrezi (see page 48), Anda Raita
   (see page 159) and ready-made parathas
>> Bhuna Gosht, Spinach Dal and Jeera Pulao
   (see the box on pages 170–1)

For dinner parties, it's more of the same, with fancier recipes and a quick dessert. I cook a few dishes in advance in large quantities and either freeze them or keep them in the fridge. I then reheat them just before the meal, either in the oven or the microwave. The trick is to leave as little to do on the day as possible.

Larger crowds and wilder soirées call for clever thinking. The simplest thing to do, I've found, is to cook large batches of filling food. Little parcels, croquettes and other bits that need to be individually fashioned and then fried are definite no-nos. The ingredients of choice for me are chicken drumsticks, potatoes, vegetables and lentils that can be grilled or left to bake while I get pretty. Laid out with some homemade chutney and flatbread, they effortlessly make me the life and soul of the party.

Cooking Extra to Save Time in the Future

Cooking for eight in order to feed two is a sub-continental cultural phenomenon. Where I come from, it is customary to feel overwhelmed by hospitality and the vast quantities of food served. Who am I to disregard years of ritual overfeeding?

In fact, this time-honoured tradition works rather well for me. If I'm going to forgo speed-dialling my local Japanese takeaway, I want to savour the results more than just once.

This means I have a special relationship with Tupperware. I buy a lot of it but deplete most of my supply by drunkenly distributing doggy bags to guests after dinner parties. Then I start stockpiling them again. My fridge contains more Tupperware than food. There are boxes filled with half-used vegetables, leftover chopped tomatoes and fresh puréed ginger and garlic paste.

We eat our fill of what was cooked the day before. The remainder gets stashed away in the freezer for another day's feast. I've worked out that you can freeze just about anything: dal, chicken curry, lamb curry and so on. But not cooked potatoes or rice. I learnt the hard way that they get horribly soggy when you defrost them at room temperature or in a microwave.

How long the stuff lasts in a freezer clearly depends on the appliance. In the knock-off, creaking freezer supplied by a penny-pinching landlord, I could wait about a month before sensibly emptying the contents of rock-solid Tupperware. In my glossy, second-hand Smeg, I give each frozen box about two months.

And each time, the food tastes even better defrosted and reheated. Firstly, because it's the flavoursome leftovers (as explained on page 35). Secondly, because I didn't have to cook it from scratch on a day when I simply didn't have the energy to do so.

WHEN AND WHAT TO DRINK WITH INDIAN FOOD   A CAUTIONARY TALE

When I gained enough confidence in the kitchen, I invited my colleagues for dinner. The drinks were flowing. Nerves (mine) were running high. I drank one glass of wine. Then another while they waited to be fed. Before I knew it, the room was spinning and the food looked as green as I felt.

Staying sober until the curry's cooked is a difficult task. I tend to join the festivities prematurely. Which inevitably leads to last-minute, bleary-eyed panic.

The odd glass of alcoholic beverage while cooking curry is a must. It fills me with the confidence of a teenage Ferrari driver. But it's hard to stop there. So when the pressure is on (i.e. my boss is waiting to be fed/colleagues are relying on my party snacks) I simply avoid drinking until the food's on the table. And overcompensate for the abstinence later.

The tipple of choice is almost always a good-quality vodka or gin. Both are non-acidic, highly distilled, refreshingly smooth and go perfectly with a dash of tonic water and Indian food. Saying that, I also consume copious amounts of wine with curry. This is not always the best idea for food cooked with yoghurt, chillies and spices. Acidic, oaky or tannin-heavy varieties are best avoided, judging from my morning-after experiences. When in doubt, I read the labels. 'Fruity' and 'easy to drink' are the buzzwords to look out for.

There's beer too. Which I know little about and avoid at all costs to save my gut from an expansive fate. When I'm buying it for guests, top choices are Asian varieties like Cobra, Kingfisher or Tiger beer. Works a treat every time.

BEFORE YOU START, REMEMBER THIS:

» OIL COOKING IN A PAN WILL SIZZLE AGAINST A WOODEN SPOON WHEN IT IS HOT AND READY FOR YOUR INGREDIENTS.

» INDIAN FOOD SMELLS GREAT BUT NOT ON YOU OR YOUR FURNITURE. PROTECT YOURSELF!

» WHACK UP THE HEAT AND STIR LIKE A MANIAC TO PREVENT FOOD FROM BURNING.

» IF THE INGREDIENTS GET STUCK TO THE BOTTOM OF THE PAN, ADD A BIT OF HOT WATER AND SCRAPE THEM OFF.

» TRY NOT TO GET DRUNK AND PASS OUT BEFORE DINNER IS READY.

2.

PERFECT IN NO TIME

Quick recipes for when you'd rather not
be in the kitchen

Miss Masala.

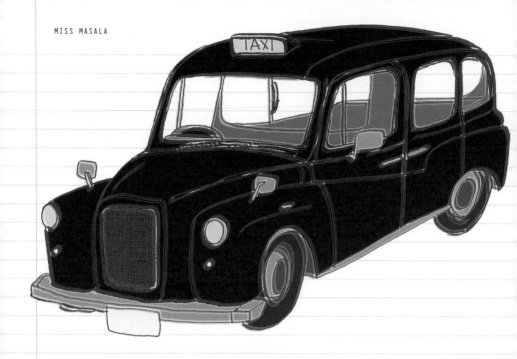

YET ANOTHER CLIENT CRISIS, the biggest new business pitch ever
and two long meetings. Being part PR consultant and part domestic goddess
can be hard going. Still sitting at my desk at eight in the evening, editing
version 25 of what was once an interesting report on a riveting subject,
I was considering professional suicide with one quick e-mail.

Dear client, I began, *much as I would like to spend the rest of my life editing your
insightful document, I no longer have the will to continue.* And then, the cleaners
arrived. It was a sign from above. My brain entered meltdown mode. I pressed
delete and started wondering what to cook for dinner as I grabbed my coat,
dashed outside and flagged down a taxi on the street.

All I needed now to unwind was an uneventful ride home and a hearty
Indian meal. It's at moments like this that I am tempted to call the local
Spice-Tandoori-Balti-Taj-Mahal-Whatever. For anything with chilli and
turmeric in it. That I don't have to cook myself.

Time seems almost always to be in short supply in my life. Cooking Indian
food has to jostle for pride of place in a topsy-turvy week of client deadlines,
unexpected guests and last-minute plans with friends. Days are mostly spent
planning evenings out with close friends at cocktail bars, restaurants or
nightclubs. And then recovering from them.

There is a time and a place for elaborate cooking. Busy weekdays and social weekends most definitely aren't it. But masala cravings can make me do terrible things. I have ghastly memories of midnight meals. Gammon steaks wrapped in ready-frozen parathas. Soda bread soaked in mango pickle. Cringe-worthy failed attempts to cook dal when drunk. I've even come this close to trying out an Australian colleague's recipe for curry porridge.

The sensible thing to do, of course, is to cook oneself something when sober and wide awake. Something requiring minimum effort but with maximum result. A wholesome, healthy dish that uses fridge-ready ingredients and takes no more than half an hour from preparation to plate.

I'm talking protein-rich vegetable dal, a comforting pulao or some bhuna chicken with salad. All cooked in extra quantities to provide sustenance before and after a booze-fuelled evening, or simply frozen for busy days to come and other desperate moments.

I racked my brains for inspiration as I flopped on to the taxi seat. The back of a black cab is usually where I pause to think and take stock. Make calendar notes of birthdays. Return overdue phone calls. Painfully remind myself of the meagre contents of the fridge.

And then the friendly driver interrupted my reverie:

'Are you Welsh?'

Here we go again …

'Indian? You speak very good English?'

It might have been the years of the Raj that clinched it.

'I love curry. Madras is my favourite.'

At which point, I flung away my CrackBerry and launched into an impassioned monologue about real Indian food. While I was at it, I handed out a 10-minute lesson in Indian history and chucked in some quick Indian cooking tips for good measure. The driver humoured me as we turned into my street.

The lecturing got me thinking. Madras and phal may be figments of the Western culinary imagination (refer to rant on page 17), but some truly authentic dishes have infiltrated British curry-house fare. And not all of them take hours of preparation and stirring. Just the way I like it.

Chicken Jhalfrezi

Pan-fried chicken with fresh green peppers

Chicken Jhalfrezi is a personal favourite. Literally meaning 'chilli fried', a jhalfrezi is an Indian stir-fry. Flummoxed? So was I when I saw the curry-house version – limp green peppers swimming in a watery marinade.

This recipe really is worth dragging the beastly Ken Hom wok from the dark underbelly of my kitchen cabinet. I set it on a high heat. Fry up lean chicken and strips of pepper and onion with the tiniest amount of oil. Rip open a bag of fresh watercress and rocket to serve it on. And say a quiet thanks for chatty cabbies.

Feeds 4
4 skinless chicken thigh fillets
4 tbsp low-fat natural yoghurt
1 tbsp tomato purée
1 tsp turmeric powder
½ tsp chilli powder
2 tbsp freshly squeezed lemon juice
2 medium onions
1 large tomato
2 green peppers
1 tbsp oil
½ tsp garlic paste
1 tsp ginger paste
1 tsp garam masala
25g (1oz) fresh coriander, roughly chopped
salt

1. Slice the chicken into strips and soak it in the yoghurt, tomato purée, turmeric and chilli, adding the lemon juice for extra zing. While it's marinating, peel the onions and slice these plus the tomato and green peppers into 1cm (½in) wide slices.

2. Warm the oil in a wok or large frying pan set over a high heat. When it sizzles, fry the onions and garlic and ginger pastes for 2–3 minutes until softened.

3. Now add the chicken, with its marinade, and stir vigorously for 5 minutes until the meat is sealed evenly. Throw in the tomato slices and keep cooking and stirring over a high heat for about 5 minutes.

4. Finally, toss in the green peppers and garam masala. Cover the wok/pan with a tight-fitting lid and cook for a further 2 minutes until the peppers soften and the chicken has absorbed its yoghurt marinade.

5. Stir in the coriander, add salt to taste and serve the chicken piled high on a bed of mixed green salad leaves tossed with fresh lemon juice, salt and chilli powder.

HOMEMADE GINGER
AND GARLIC PASTES

OKAY, HERE'S THE TRUTH.
The one thing I keep failing to achieve is jars of fresh,
lovingly prepared homemade ginger and garlic paste. I usually
purée the amount I need for a recipe just before I get started.
One fat clove of garlic and 1cm ($\frac{1}{2}$in) root ginger gives
approximately 2 teaspoons of ginger-garlic paste when puréed
with 1 tablespoon of water.

Jars of store-bought garlic and ginger pastes are a
permanent fixture in my fridge for those exceptionally lazy
days. If you can be slightly more organised than me, by all
means make your own. Twelve fat garlic cloves peeled and puréed
in a hand blender with 2 tablespoons of water will give you
12 teaspoons of garlic paste. For ginger, 15cm (6in) peeled root
ginger puréed with 2 tablespoons of water will give you about
12 teaspoons of the paste. Seal them tight in well-washed
and thoroughly dried glass jars (I reuse empty ginger and
garlic paste bottles) and use for up to four days,
keeping them in the fridge.

TO MARINATE
OR NOT TO MARINATE

Leaving meat to sit for hours is not absolutely
essential, but the longer you give it, the more flavoursome
and tender it becomes. Plan shopping trips, makeup application
and household chores to take place after you've whipped
up the marinade, to make best use of time.

Aloo Gobi

Famous sautéed potato and cauliflower

Aloo Gobi was immortalised in Gurinder Chadha's *Bend It Like Beckham*. My mother, unlike her counterpart in the film, would have me turning professional footballer any day over queen of authentic Aloo Gobi. Thankfully, I don't play football. Which means I am free to hold forth in the back of black cabs, extolling the virtues of this celebrated north Indian dish.

A classic bhuna or stirred dish, Aloo Gobi is cooked in its own juices and best made with the freshest vegetables. Serve it tucked into warm toasted pitta bread.

Feeds 4

Vegetarian
400g (14oz) cauliflower
4 large new potatoes
1 small onion
1cm (½in) root ginger
1 garlic clove
2 tbsp oil
1 tsp coriander powder
1 tsp cumin powder
¼ tsp turmeric powder
½ tsp chilli powder
1 tsp garam masala
1 large handful of fresh
  coriander, roughly chopped
salt

1. First cut the cauliflower into large bite-sized florets. This will prevent them from falling apart once they start cooking. Peel and quarter the potatoes and peel and finely chop the onion, ginger and garlic.

2. Warm the oil in a large frying pan set over a high heat. When it starts to sizzle, add the onions, garlic and ginger and fry for about 5 minutes until they soften and turn translucent. Next, throw in the potatoes and all the spices, apart from the garam masala.

3. Add a tablespoon of water, cover the pan with a lid and partly cook the potatoes for 5–10 minutes. When you can insert a fork into them, but with some difficulty, it's time to add the cauliflower florets. It's crucial not to add the cauliflower too early, however – you don't want it to overcook!

4. Once you've added the cauliflower, stir well to incorporate with the other ingredients, cover the pan once again and cook for 3–4 minutes until the florets are soft but still whole.

5. Sprinkle the garam masala all over, add salt to taste and finish with a handful of chopped coriander.

Palak Paneer
Indian cheese in a spiced spinach purée

By far the most popular recipe on my blog, and it's no surprise why: soft chunks of paneer and spiced spinach purée are a match made in heaven and the last thing I will eat if I ever find myself on the way to hell.

Fresh spinach works just fine in this recipe. But why bother, when freshly frozen spinach is more nutritious and is almost always sitting in a big bag in the freezer. Make loads in one go – you'll crave this for at least two days afterwards.

Feeds 4

Vegetarian
225g (8oz) paneer
½ tsp turmeric powder
½ tsp chilli powder
1 medium onion
4 garlic cloves
2.5cm (1in) root ginger
2 tbsp oil
1 large fresh green
 finger chilli
1 tsp cumin powder
500g (1lb 2oz) frozen spinach
½ tsp garam masala
salt

1. Chop the block of paneer into even, bite-sized pieces. In a large bowl, mix the paneer pieces with the turmeric and chilli and a teaspoon of salt, then set aside.

2. Now, peel and roughly chop the onion, then peel and purée the ginger and garlic with a hand blender. Pour the oil into a large non-stick frying pan and set over a high heat. When the oil is hot, add the paneer and fry on one side until golden brown and then flip the pieces over and repeat on the opposite side. Remove the paneer with a slotted spoon and place back in the bowl.

3. In the same frying pan and using the oil left in the pan, fry the onions, ginger and garlic. While these are cooking, roughly chop the chilli. When the onions start going translucent, after about 5 minutes, mix in the cumin and the chilli. Fry for a further 5 minutes until the mixture turns a deep golden brown.

4. Now mix in the frozen spinach and let it cook for 5 minutes. When it is thoroughly defrosted in the pan and evenly mixed with the masala, add half a mug of hot water and go in with a hand blender to liquidise the whole lot into a smooth, creamy mixture. Alternatively, you could whiz the spinach in a food processor for the same result. »

5. When the spinach mixture is smooth, pour it back into the pan, then add the fried paneer pieces and the garam masala. Lower the heat and simmer for 10 minutes until all the liquid has evaporated and the spinach has absorbed the spices evenly (taste a little just to check).

6. At this point, add salt to taste. You'll need to add a fair bit to offset the blandness of the spinach. But this dish is worth it. Eat it piping hot as a side dish or with some ready-made naans for a complete meal.

I ARRIVED HOME FROM WORK FEELING INSPIRED. Ready to roll my sleeves up and set the pots on the fire. But it's never quite that simple. I first had to change into a retro nightdress (for which, read 'old, torn'), pour myself a vodka lemonade and fire up the laptop. The urgent pleas of desperate new converts to Indian cooking around the world required an immediate response on my Quick Indian Cooking blog:

Help, I have no raisins! Done.
Do you have a single sister? Ignore.
Would you like to enlarge your penis? Bin.

Before I knew it, it was time for dinner. The options were limited. Since my university days, I've avoided greasy takeaways like a double helping of lard. So we could eat one of the three dishes my man had perfected. Or something low in fat and high in wonderful things I hastily offered to put together instead.

But this just wasn't good enough for some people. My half-British, half-Peruvian man is apparently a qualified authority on everything curry-related. Now he was hungry and smarting from rejection. Between quick cigarette drags out on the balcony, he slunk around in my shadow, watching my every move. Whacking the flame up when I wasn't looking. Or chucking an extra green chilli into the bubbling pot.

I exploded momentarily. Then rolled my eyes and poured myself another stiff drink. Food would be ready soon. Gok Wan was about to take on the new season's fashion trends. Kitchen squabbles will pass, I reminded myself. All I needed now was a plate of food and a remote control.

The man sensed a power struggle. He piled his plate high with whatever was in the pot and rushed to the couch, clutching the remote for dear life. Then I heard a wail of protest from the living room: 'There's no ghee in this!' Turned out this curry-loving, Cobra Beer-drinking Latino is also a superlative judge of the adequate level of fat in dal.

Fat and health are serious issues in my home. Most Indians I know speak of cholesterol, high blood pressure and adult acne with the reverence ordinarily reserved for national security and socio-economic issues. My family home in India was particularly full of health freaks. Mother kept cooking oil under lock and key. Our cook, Dada, schemed to sneak vegetables into every dish. Dad treated deep-fried foods like post-war rations. And even the dog rejected red meat.

I value my size eight bod too much to feel otherwise. Besides, I also work in public relations. The office is full of gorgeous blondes on size-zero diets. Bread and bananas are conspicuously absent. The beauties to my right pay daily tribute to the canned tuna and bagged salad industries. With my two-course curry lunches and chocolate biscuit habits, a few teaspoons of oil is the only guilty pleasure I can afford at home.

I use measured amounts of oil in everyday Indian cooking. Deep-frying is strictly banned in my home. Where it offers a suitable alternative to shallow-frying, I bake or grill dishes. But call me weak; I just can't resist a dash of sublime buttery ghee in a pot of thick, piping-hot dal.

Now, I was being accused of playing miser with that promised teaspoon of liquid gold. I briefly contemplated knocking the man out with the can of ghee. Luckily for him, it was too much effort for me. I sighed and curled up on the couch with my own mound of well-deserved dinner. Ready to watch Gok Wan's pearls of fashion wisdom on TV. Ready for the rest.

COOKING OILS

LOVE IT OR HATE IT,
YOU CAN'T COOK INDIAN FOOD WITHOUT OIL.

When I started cooking while studying for my journalism degree, I failed spectacularly to make Indian food using miniscule quantities of oil. It was devastating to accept that I'd be old and wrinkled before three onions would fry in one teaspoon of oil. So I compromised by using non-stick pans and as little oil as was necessary to cook the food properly. At the time my journalism tutors joked: 'Never believe anything written in newspapers.' I haven't quite followed this sound advice. Some article glorified the health benefits of sunflower oil and I've used it in Indian cooking ever since.

In truth, I could use any flavourless, colourless variety of oil that has a high smoking point, such as corn, groundnut or safflower oil. These are what I recommend for my recipes unless I specify otherwise. There's also coconut oil, used widely in south India, and mustard oil, popular in Bengal. But I use these only occasionally. Mainly because I can never find storage space for them in my kitchen cupboards.

And finally, there's olive oil.
A contentious choice - fast becoming most fashionable in India. But let me ask you, would you cook a pasta dish with mustard oil? Or a roast dinner in coconut oil? Besides, olive oil loses its famous delicate flavour when heated to the high temperatures needed for Indian cooking, and it costs a bomb. So wrong on so many levels. Best avoided for curries, I say.

Tadka Dal
Buttery lentils with vegetables and sizzling cumin

Dal and rice is easily the simplest and healthiest Indian meal to cook. Masoor dal, or split red lentils, are my all-time favourite because they cook quickly and are readily available in virtually any supermarket or corner shop.

High protein content aside, this is the ultimate comfort food. Think hangover cure meets warm soft cuddle. This dish is incomplete without the tablespoon of ghee that makes it so sublimely buttery. Just chuck in some raw peas, carrots and cauliflower to appease your guilty conscience.

Feeds 4

Vegetarian
200g (7oz) masoor
  (split red) lentils
½ tsp turmeric powder
1 large tomato
200g (7oz) chopped raw
  vegetables, such as green
  beans, carrots, peas and
  cauliflower
1 tbsp ghee
1 pinch of asafoetida
2 dried long red chillies
½ tsp chilli powder
1 tsp cumin seeds
salt

1. Wash the lentils under a cold tap until the water runs clean. In a medium pan, mix these with the turmeric, then add twice as much cold water as lentils and bring to the boil. Once the water starts bubbling rapidly, lower the heat to medium. Stir the lentils every 5 minutes to prevent them from settling on the bottom or sides of the pan.

2. Watch the pan, skimming off any foam that rises to the surface. If the lentils threaten to boil over, take the pan off the heat for a few seconds. If they have soaked up all the water, add a half mug of hot water to keep the mixture fluid.

3. After about 20 minutes, the lentils will slowly disintegrate and resemble a fibrous soup. When this happens, roughly chop the tomato and add it to the pan, stirring over the heat for about 5 minutes until the tomato starts to melt into the lentils. Now stir in the raw vegetables that you are using. They'll cook with the lentils, sealing their natural goodness in the dal.

4. Stir gently for about 10 more minutes until the vegetables are done and the lentils have formed a thick, golden-yellow soup. Add salt to taste and leave to simmer over a low heat while you make the tadka. »

5. Warm the ghee on a high heat in the smallest pan you possess. When it starts to sizzle, add the asafoetida, long red chillies, chilli powder and cumin seeds. Within seconds, the spices will start spluttering and releasing their heady aromas. Take the pan off the heat and stir the tadka into the lentil mixture.

6. Pour the piping-hot dal over fluffy basmati rice and enjoy with mango pickle and papads.

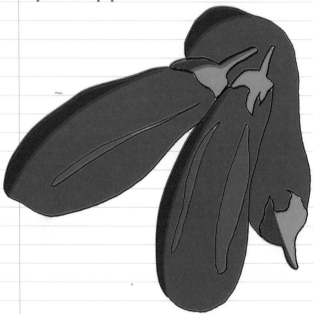

INTRODUCING AJWAIN

AJWAIN, or carom fruit pods, resemble little greyish seeds and add a pungent and slightly bitter tangy edge to dishes. They are an essential pickling spice and taste lovely sprinkled sparingly over summer salads.

Achari Baingan
Aubergine baked with tangy pickling spices

Health and fat content become even more serious issues as beach holidays approach. The more I visualise myself in a tiny bikini, the more I feel like a washed-up Bay of Bengal whale. Last-minute weight reduction calls for different thinking and drastic solutions.

That's how I came up with this low-fat twist on a popular Madhur Jaffrey recipe. Hers calls for aubergine and potatoes to be pre-fried before further cooking. I just leave the potatoes out and bake the whole lot instead. This is also a great dish to serve guests, as it just cooks in the oven while you get on with other stuff.

Feeds 2
Vegetarian
2 medium aubergines
1 tsp chilli powder
1 tsp turmeric powder
1 tsp oil
1 tsp nigella seeds
1 tsp fennel seeds
1 tsp ajwain seeds
1 x 200g can of chopped
    tomatoes
salt

shallow rectangular
ovenproof dish

1. Preheat the oven to 220°C (425°F), gas mark 7.

2. Thickly slice and then quarter the aubergine into bite-sized chunks. Mix these with the chilli, turmeric and some salt in a large bowl.

3. Spread the oil over base of the ovenproof dish. Add the whole spices to the dish and cook in the oven for 1 minute until they start to roast and give off their lovely aromas.

4. Now tip the aubergine mixture into the dish, empty the can of chopped tomatoes into it and mix well. Add a little salt if needed.

5. Bake in the centre of the oven for 30 minutes, stirring halfway through cooking, until the aubergines are cooked but still intact. The tinned tomatoes will develop a chutney-like consistency. Serve alongside toasted wholemeal bread or warm rotis.

ABOVE Naan (page 106)

TOP Aloo Gobi (page 50)
ABOVE Kolmino Patio (page 70)

ABOVE Masala Fish (page 60)

Masala Fish

Grilled rainbow trout with lemon, coriander and chilli

As a little girl, I had bad eyesight and wore thick pink-rimmed spectacles aged barely eight. The cure, according to the local optician, was to eat fish. Lots of it. This was a sign from above for my Bengali fish-loving family, who proceeded to force-feed me the stuff. Little bones and all.

Twenty-odd years later, I am virtually blind in both eyes. But I do see the nutritional sense in eating fish, if not quite as obsessively as I was made to as a child. I've particularly warmed to the idea of grilled fish on a weekday. Along with fillets of salmon and cod, rainbow trout is a regular purchase. It's high in omega 3 and available all year round, conveniently cleaned and sealed on a supermarket shelf.

Feeds 2

2 whole rainbow trout, gutted
100g (3½oz) fresh coriander leaves (a large bunch)
4 fresh green finger chillies
4 garlic cloves
4 tbsp mustard oil
freshly squeezed juice of 1 lemon
salt

1. Preheat the grill to medium. Wash the trout well and make three shallow sideways slits on one side of each of them.

2. In a blender or food processor, purée all the remaining ingredients together. Coat the fish evenly with the thick green marinade and grill for 10 minutes on each side.

3. Serve with a salad of cucumber, onion and tomato tossed in freshly squeezed lemon juice.

I'D BE LYING IF I CLAIMED TO WORK LATE EVERY NIGHT.

Most weekday evenings, I sit at my desk like a bored schoolgirl, waiting impatiently for the clock to strike six. Then I extract a makeup palette from my stationery drawer and paint on a new face. Ready to embrace whatever complex social arrangement I have made.

It could be a few quick drinks in Soho with friends. A three-course dinner with former colleagues. Maybe sushi and a play with a close girlfriend. Or an impromptu drink with the team at work.

I slipped out for a quick gossip over wine with a former colleague one weekday recently. The plan didn't involve a full meal. The venue was a trendy gastropub, nestled between two popular theatres. It was all low lighting and walnut furniture. Men in suits were draped over the bar area. Women wearing boots over skinny jeans were eyeing each other up between margaritas and murmurs.

Desperate for seating, we balanced ourselves on midget-sized leather stools arranged around a tree-trunk table. Hoped we wouldn't get stepped on. And then sensibly got going with a large glass of Merlot each and complementary mixed nuts. When the second glass arrived, we ordered a portion of olives. And midway through that, *what the hell*, we got stuck into a bowl of thick-cut fries. All the while talking holidays, massages and bosses. We'd agreed on an early night and went our different ways. Now it was past dinner time and I would have to fend for myself.

On the tube home, I thought about all the different things I could cook quickly. Walked towards the flat praying for a bursting fridge – or even a semi-bursting one. Ran up the stairs, starving. Flung open the fridge. And found it virtually empty.

There is nothing worse than coming home starving to find the fridge empty.

Bar one item, that is. I stood with the Smeg door open, frost in my face; staring with disbelief at the pack of mince I'd been saving for Keema Mattar. It had expired two days ago. Surely the Food Standards Agency had a solution for this? I reached for the bin, and a vision of my bossy Nani flashed before me: 'Tsk, tsk, think of all the starving children back in India.'

Desperate, I rummaged through half-eaten packs of vegetables, pantry tins and freezer bags. Normally, there is something I can defrost and eat. But I was having no such luck. There must be some ingredients I could quickly transform into an instant curry? My freezer was heaving with packs of curry leaves, coriander and mint. The kitchen cupboard had a wealth of canned legumes and meagre supplies of ginger, garlic, tomatoes and onions.

Recipes for vegetable and legume curries are the answer in moments like this. The rules of engagement are flexible. I had an assortment of ingredients that would work magic together. For everything else, there was the corner shop, open late.

I had found a solution. It would be perfect in no time.

Navratan Korma
Nine 'jewels' in a creamy nutty curry

This thick and creamy curry can be a major rescue operation for neglected vegetables. The nine ingredients (the 'nine gems' or 'navratan') you use is a moveable feast. Down south it is cooked with lots of coconut, but this is the north Indian version, which uses yoghurt and milk to thicken the curry base. Don't be put off by the lengthy list of ingredients – even my husband can cook this.

Feeds 4

Vegetarian
2 large onions
3 tbsp oil
125g (4½oz) paneer
1 small handful of raisins, blanched almonds and cashew nuts
2 tsp ginger paste
1 tsp garlic paste
1 tbsp tomato purée
½ tsp chilli powder
½ tsp turmeric powder
1 tsp coriander powder
½ tsp cumin powder
600ml (1 pint) semi-skimmed milk
200g (7oz) natural Greek yoghurt
3 large handfuls of pre-prepared vegetables, such as peas, carrots and potatoes (peeled and chopped, green beans, cauliflower (cut into florets)
½ tsp garam masala
salt

1. Warm a tablespoon of oil in a small frying pan set over a high heat. Chop the paneer into bite-sized cubes and, when the oil is hot, sauté with the raisins and nuts until the mixture is toffee brown. Remove from the heat and set aside.

2. Peel and chop the onions into tiny pieces. Add the remaining oil to a large pan set over a high heat. When it starts sizzling, add the chopped onion and ginger and garlic pastes. Fry vigorously for 10 minutes until the whole lot turns a pale golden colour.

3. Now add the tomato purée and the spice powders apart from the garam masala. Fry for another 5 minutes until oil starts oozing out of the masala mixture.

4. Lower the heat to medium and stir in the milk and yoghurt. Mix thoroughly so that the mixture doesn't split or curdle. Cook for about 5 minutes until combined.

5. Now add each of the vegetables according to the time they will need to cook. Hence the carrots and potatoes go in first, for 15 minutes, followed by the cauliflower, beans and peas, for 3–4 minutes, until the whole lot is cooked.

6. Stir in the paneer, nuts and raisins along with the oil they were cooked in and the garam masala, and simmer for a final 2 minutes. Add salt to taste and serve with ready-made naans for an instant, vegetarian feast.

Rajma
Super-simple and healthy kidney bean curry

Rajma is one of the easiest and most satisfying north Indian dishes. A heaped bowl of rice served with this wholesome kidney bean curry is all I need before I settle in front of the TV for the evening.

It should come as no surprise that I use a can of drained ready-cooked kidney beans for this recipe. Go wild and spend an extra 20 pence on the organic version, with no added sugar or salt.

Feeds 2
Vegetarian
1 small onion
1 large tomato
1 tbsp oil
whole spices
  1 bay leaf
  4 cardamoms
  4 cloves
  2.5cm (1in) cinnamon stick
2 tsp ginger paste
1 tsp garlic paste
2 tsp coriander powder
2 tsp cumin powder
½ tsp freshly ground black
  pepper
½ tsp chilli powder
1 tsp turmeric powder
1 x 400g can kidney beans
½ tsp garam masala
salt

1. Peel the onion and chop it and the tomato into little pieces. Pour the oil into a medium pan set over a high heat. When it's hot, add the whole spices. As they sizzle up, stir in the onion and ginger and garlic pastes and fry until golden brown.

2. Next add all the powdered spices, apart from the garam masala powder. Stir-fry for 5 minutes and then chuck in the chopped tomato.

3. Fry this masala mixture for 5 minutes until the pungent aroma of the spices softens. Then add water to cover, lower the heat and simmer until you see oil oozing from little pores in the mixture. Jab the mixture with a wooden spoon at regular intervals until you have a pastelike texture.

4. Now, rinse and drain the kidney beans and add to the masala. Stir, add water to cover, and simmer for 10 minutes until the onions disintegrate. Mash 10–15 kidney beans against the sides of the pan to thicken the curry. To finish, mix in the garam masala and a little salt.

Channa Masala
Hot, spiced bhuna chickpeas

Channa, or chickpeas, are like leggy blondes in trendy nightclubs – cheap, bland and readily available. But all dressed up they're unrecognisable. Chickpeas are nutritious, easy to cook and yummy spiced up with tomatoes, chillies and tangy amchoor, or mango powder (see the box overleaf).

Channa Masala is versatile enough to be eaten as a main dish or enjoyed alongside dal and keema. But I must confess – I never have the time to cook raw chickpeas. For me, they're the ultimate fast food. Out of a 42-pence can, rinsed, drained and thrown straight into masala.

Feeds 2

Vegetarian
1 large onion
2 large tomatoes
2 tbsp oil
1 tsp cumin seeds
1 tbsp garlic paste
1 tbsp ginger paste
4 tsp coriander powder
2 tsp cumin powder
1 tsp chilli powder
2 x 400g cans of chickpeas
1 tsp garam masala
1 tsp amchoor powder
25g fresh coriander,
    chopped
salt

1. Peel and finely chop the onion and cut the tomatoes into little pieces. Pour the oil in a medium pan set over a high heat. When it starts to sizzle, add the cumin seeds and the onions. Fry for about 5 minutes until the onions soften and turn translucent. Stir in the ginger and garlic pastes and fry for a further 5 minutes or so until the mixture begins to brown.

2. Next stir in all the masala powders, saving the garam masala and amchoor for later, until the pungent aromas of the raw spices give way to something more delicate and irresistible. Now pour in half a mug of hot water and watch the masala mixture bubble up. Let it cook until the water has evaporated.

3. Stir in the chopped tomatoes and stir-fry for 2 minutes until they melt away into the rest of the mixture. Then lower the heat to medium and simmer for a further 5 minutes until the masala really starts to thicken. When this happens, rinse and drain the chickpeas, and tip them in. Give them a good stir, adding another half mug of hot water and the garam masala. 》

4. Simmer gently for about 10 minutes until the oil begins to reappear on the surface of the channa, and all the water has been absorbed.

5. Sprinkle over the amchoor and chopped coriander to finish, adding salt to taste. This is great with some oven-baked naans topped with a knob of butter.

INTRODUCING AMCHOOR

Amchoor, dried raw mango powder, adds a tangy twist to vegetable curries and salads. Sprinkle a little on a dish at the end of cooking to enjoy its fresh zesty taste.

SPEED COOKING

WHEN ALL ELSE FAILS, THESE MEALTIME MASALA HITS RISE TO THE OCCASION:

>> Cooked ready-frozen parathas with natural Greek yoghurt and mango pickle.
>> Cod or salmon fillet doused in fresh lemon juice, chilli powder, turmeric and a little salt, and popped under the grill.
>> Scrambled eggs – well cooked and not runny – with finely chopped onions, sliced tomatoes and chopped green finger chillies, served on toast with chilli sauce.

THE STRESS OF FINDING THE FRIDGE BARE and having to

cobble together a speedy dinner for myself pales into insignificance when it comes to needing to impress a last-minute guest with an apparently effortless Indian meal.

Finally, I had a quiet weekday evening ahead of me. Deadlines had been met. Social engagements avoided. I was looking forward to going home and putting my feet up on the Barcelona stool. I had opted to eat something semi-virtuous that could be scraped out of a jar. Then I got that phone call. Did I have plans for the evening?

Not until a second ago I didn't. Now I had an impromptu dinner guest, coming over for quality female bonding over career dilemmas, relationship troubles and flatmate nightmares. I was going to be the voice of reason sounding through a fog of muddled thoughts. Hurrah! My evening had a sense of purpose after all.

I grabbed a free newspaper en route to the pricey neighbourhood convenience store. Page 30 had an interesting quick supper suggestion of Black Paella. It needed mixed seafood, paella rice, peppers. And squid ink! After working hours? Who writes this drivel?

I binned the rag. I had a cupboard bursting with exotic Indian spices. They would have to do. A quick call home to the man to alert him to changed arrangements for the evening and to confirm Smeg-ready ingredients. I bought the bare minimum top-up ingredients and alcohol, then headed home.

If I was to dissect deep, meaningful and complex issues, I needed to get fiddly chores out of the way. The minute I entered the flat, frantic preparation commenced. I opened the windows wide. Changed into semi-respectable casual wear (i.e. not torn or faded). Minced onions in my little chopper. Diced the meat. Sliced my finger. Flew around the place looking for a plaster. While cursing knives and meat curry.

As dinner finally got going, my friend arrived. We had only a couple of hours on a school night. My attention was to be divided between matters of great significance – my friend's emotional wellbeing and dinner bubbling away on the hob. It was a fine balance. A close friendship was at stake on the one hand. My personal reputation as a burgeoning Indian cooking talent on the other.

I quickly shoved a dish into the oven to finish it off and poured us some vodka. Dinner comprised two dishes only, Kolmino Patio and Dal Palak, but containing the fanciest ingredients I was able to source in a rush. My pressure cooker was on standby should I start running out of time. We sat at the kitchen table, talking, stirring and then eating. With enough alcohol to keep us going. And no stress to impress.

A MEATY QUESTION

WHAT CUTS OF MEAT ARE BEST TO USE IN INDIAN COOKING? THE PRINCIPLES ARE SIMPLE:

>> Chicken on the bone only, apart from skinless and boneless thigh meat. Chicken breast is virtually impenetrable by a masala unless marinated and tenderised for hours.

>> Cheaper cuts of lamb like neck fillet and diced shoulder soak spices and soften up beautifully in a curry. Stash the more expensive leg of lamb away for roast dinners.

>> Lamb chunks can be replaced with lean stewing beef, although this isn't eaten by Hindus in India.

>> In India, goat is the meat of choice for curries. More tender than lamb when cooked, but sans the strong smell. Only worth trying from a reputable Halal butcher, though.

Kerala Chicken Curry
Aromatic chicken with curry leaves and coconut

Coconut milk and curry leaves are a staple of south Indian cuisine. There's something magical about creamy liquid coconut combined with the sharp curry aroma of the fresh leaves. This dish is guaranteed to make my man go weak at the knees and hand over his credit card.

Of course, a tin of coconut milk is about as fatty as a tub of double cream. And far more devilishly divine. This is my reduced-fat version of the dish – with a bit of clever thinking and no compromise on taste.

Feeds 4

500g (1lb 2oz) skinless chicken thigh fillets
1 large onion
2 tbsp oil
1 tsp fennel seeds
4 whole black peppercorns
10 fresh or frozen curry leaves
2 tsp garlic paste
1 tsp ginger paste
½ tsp chilli powder
½ tsp turmeric powder
4 tsp coriander powder
4 small new potatoes
1 medium tomato
4 small shallots
200ml (7fl oz) reduced-fat coconut milk
½ tsp garam masala
salt

1. Cut the chicken into bite-sized chunks and peel and finely chop the onion. Pour the oil into a large pan set over a high heat. When it's hot, add the fennel seeds, peppercorns and curry leaves.

2. As they sizzle up, mix in the chopped onion and the ginger and garlic pastes. Fry the whole lot for 10 minutes, stirring regularly, until the mixture turns a pale gold in colour, and then stir in all the powdered spices apart from the garam masala.

3. Fry this lot for a further 5 minutes, stirring regularly. You want the smell of the masala to soften from strong and raw to a more subtle aroma. In the meantime, halve the new potatoes, slice the tomato and peel and chop the shallots.

4. Next, stir the chicken cubes into the masala mixture. Brown the chicken on all sides, then stir in the coconut milk, potatoes and tomato. Lower the heat to medium and let it all cook for 10 minutes.

5. Finally, set the heat to low and chuck in the shallots, garam masala and salt to taste. Simmer for 2 minutes until a little oil starts appearing on the surface, and then serve hot with plain steamed rice.

Kolmino Patio
Prawns in a spicy, sweet and sour curry

The Parsi community – originally Persians who emigrated to the west of India – are renowned for their flavoursome cuisine. I have vivid memories of parties at my close Parsi friend's home in India, where dishes of spicy pomfret (a type of fish), prawn and lamb were served with sweetened pulaos.

Kolmino Patio is a popular Parsi dish made with small prawns. I buy large bags of frozen raw, cleaned king prawns from the Oriental supermarkets in Soho. These shrink to half their size anyway when cooked. Just dunk them in warm water to defrost them before you start cooking.

Feeds 4
4 garlic cloves
1 tsp cumin seeds
½ tsp coriander seeds
4 dried red chillies
1½ tsp turmeric powder
2 tbsp oil
1 medium onion
20 raw shelled king prawns
1 tbsp tamarind paste
1 tbsp dark muscovado sugar
25g (1oz) fresh coriander, roughly chopped
salt

1. Peel the garlic cloves and then, using a hand blender, grind them to a smooth paste with the four spices and half a mug of water.

2. Warm the oil in a medium pan set over a high heat. When the oil is heating, peel and chop the onion, then add to the pan and fry for about 5 minutes, or until golden brown. Next, add the blended masala and stir with the onions for a further 5 minutes.

3. Now chuck in the prawns and cook for 2 minutes until they have turned pink. Mix in the tamarind paste, the sugar, chopped coriander and salt to taste.

4. Serve with a simple Khichdi (see page 194) and some papads.

Dal Palak
Lentils cooked with spinach and aromatic garlic

A dressed-up dal is a great accessory to an impromptu fancy meal. It still takes no time to cook, but makes a fine impression alongside steaming hot rice, pickle and papads. This spinach and lentil dal is steeped with the heady aroma of garlic. A favoured option when I'm staying put indoors.

You can tweak the basic recipe to make different versions of the same dal. For instance, add more garlic to make it a Lasuni Dal Palak, or a teaspoon of chopped ginger to balance the garlicky taste.

Feeds 4
Vegetarian
50g (2oz) moong (split yellow) lentils
50g (2oz) masoor (split red) lentils
½ tsp turmeric powder
4 garlic cloves
1 small onion
1 medium tomato
1 tbsp oil
½ tsp cumin seeds
4 cubes frozen spinach
1 tsp ghee
½ tsp chilli powder
freshly squeezed lemon juice
salt

1. Wash the lentils thoroughly, place in a medium pan and cover the lentils with twice as much cold water. Add the turmeric and bring to the boil.

2. Peel and finely chop two of the garlic cloves, peel and slice the onion and chop the tomato. Pour the oil into a small pan set over a high heat. When it's hot, add the cumin and garlic. As they sizzle up, stir in the tomato and onion and fry for 5 minutes until softened.

3. Next add the spinach, lower the heat to medium and cook until defrosted. Keep an eye on the lentils, adding a little hot water if they start to dry up. To keep the dal thick, don't add too much water, just a little bit every time the lentils start spluttering because they're getting too dry.

4. When the lentils are fully incorporated and have become souplike in consistency, stir in the spinach masala mixture. Add a little hot water to combine all the ingredients and keep the dal bubbling to let the flavours infuse.

5. After about 5 minutes, melt the ghee in a small pan set over a high heat, and peel and slice the remaining two garlic cloves. When the ghee is hot, add the garlic and the chilli powder. As the garlic starts turning golden brown, mix this tadka into the dal.

6. Stir in the lemon juice, add salt to taste and serve with basmati rice.

71

AS THE WEEKEND APPROACHES, plans become more ambitious.

Low-key weekday evenings usually give way to more glamorous late-nighters. Birthday and farewell parties, fancy restaurant dinners and drinks with friends in cocktail lounges.

I had been looking forward to my friend's 30th for weeks. I rushed home from work at the earliest opportunity. There was to be no vegetating in front of the TV that evening. I was off to her birthday drinks bash in Fulham. The corner of a nightspot had been duly reserved for an evening of vodka cocktails, crazy dance moves and drunken chit-chat. But I couldn't venture out until I had cooked a massive Indian meal that would line the stomach before the evening commenced, feed my aching belly in the wee hours of the night and triple up as breakfast the next morning.

The choice of dish was tricky. I could cook just one before I showered, changed, sorted my outfit, applied makeup and hit the party. There was no time for a blow-dry or last-minute manicure. I had to plan carefully for what lay ahead. Donning my oldest pair of pyjamas and a manky hotel-acquired shower cap, I started preparing the simple, low-smell recipe I'd chosen to see me through the night.

The dish was progressing as planned. Leaving it to bubble away on the cooker, I slipped off to iron the caramel gold top I had picked to wear with white skinnies. Whistling softly to the *Ministry of Sound Annual* and momentarily forgetting about my low-glamour look, I stepped on to the balcony. And horror of horrors, our trendy gay neighbour caught my eye from the flowerbed he was watering in the communal garden below.

This was like being caught with my knickers down. My gay neighbours think I'm the best thing that happened to them since Teri Hatcher made it on *Desperate Housewives*.

Hosepipe in hand, the record company executive raised an eyebrow: *What happened to you, dear?* I smiled back nervously: *It isn't me; it's my ugly older sister.* Mumbling an apology, I stepped back into the kitchen. Thankfully, dinner was ready to be served. I yelled 'Honeeeeeeey!' across the apartment to extract the man from the third repeat of *Top Gear* and jumped into the shower. Half an hour later, I emerged all dressed up like a Christmas tree and wolfed down the meal.

There was only one last thing left to do before we made for the bar. I had to regain my confidence. Re-establish the glamour stakes in our mansion block. I knocked on my neighbour's door in full costume and asked him a vague question about the state of the wall creepers this spring. He commented on how wonderful I looked.

I was ready to dance my feet off in four-inch gold stilettos.

PATIENCE IS A VIRTUE

... BUT SADLY NOT ONE OF MINE. HERE ARE THE TOP BAD HABITS THAT I NEED TO BREAK:

>> Stirring rice too much – No wonder I sometimes end up with a starchy mess instead of fluffy grains of perfection.

>> Wandering off – Dry ingredients left unattended to cook over a high heat can only mean burnt masala.

>> Adding spices before the onions have browned – This always means crunchy onions later. Nice

Zafrani Gosht
Tender lamb stewed in yoghurt with a hint of saffron

This stupendous lamb stew just bubbles away as I chat with friends or get ready for a big night out. The best thing is that it is low-smell. I can stir it in between showering, getting changed and applying makeup without the smallest worry that I'll end up stinking like a halal butcher.

It uses one of my favourite ingredients – yoghurt. Why favourite? It's a great low-fat substitute for cream, thickens curries and softens meats naturally. Just use a thick variety like Greek yoghurt, brought to room temperature first to prevent it from splitting the minute it's heated up.

Feeds 4
2 large onions
2 tbsp oil
whole spices
  2 dried long red chillies
  1 brown cardamom
  1 bay leaf
1 tsp garlic paste
2 tsp ginger paste
2 tsp coriander powder
250g (9oz) natural Greek
  yoghurt
800g (1¾lb) diced lamb
10 strands of saffron
salt

1. Peel and finely slice the onions. Pour the oil into a large pan set over a high heat. When it's very hot, add the whole spices and, as they sizzle, mix in the sliced onions.

2. Fry the onions for 10 minutes until they turn a pale golden brown. Then stir in the ginger and garlic pastes and fry for a further 5 minutes until the mixture caramelises to a darker shade of gold.

3. Now add the coriander powder, yoghurt and lamb and stir like a maniac, cooking the meat on all sides until it is well sealed. Add a mug of hot water – enough to submerge the meat – cover with a lid and cook on a high heat for about 30 minutes.

4. You will need to stir the curry very frequently to prevent the lamb from burning or sticking to the bottom of the pan. If it does stick, just add a little more hot water. If you're the proud owner of a pressure cooker, by all means use it. But the taste of this delicate dish comes from being cooked for the full length of time.

5. After 30 minutes, remove the lid and adjust the heat to medium–low. In another 15 minutes the lamb will be tender and virtually melt in the mouth. Then mix in the saffron strands and salt to taste, simmer for a further minute and serve piping hot with some ready-made naans.

Chicken Pulao
Fragrant rice cooked with chicken

Not just a party-night treat, pulao is to Indians what fried rice is to the Chinese. Aromatic and flavoursome, it's the perfect one-pot rice dish for a quiet night's supper at home, and a brilliant way to dress up a simple curry.

Serve the pulao steaming hot the first time you serve it, with some raita and spicy mixed pickle. Straight off the hob with a lazy spoon of natural Greek yoghurt late at night. And with anything you can stomach the morning after. Simply wonderful. Enough said

Feeds 4 (many times)
3 tbsp oil
2 medium onions
whole spices
  1 star anise
  2 tsp cumin seeds
  5cm (2in) cinnamon stick
  2 large bay leaves
1 tsp ginger paste
1 tsp garlic paste
1 tsp turmeric powder
4 fresh green finger chillies
6 skinless chicken thighs
  and drumsticks
250g (9oz) natural,
  low-fat yoghurt
350g (12oz) rice
salt

1. Pour the oil into a large pan set over a high heat and, while it is heating, peel and slice the onions. When the oil is hot, add the whole spices. As they sizzle up, chuck in the chopped onions and fry for 10 minutes until golden brown.

2. Add the ginger and garlic pastes and fry for a further 5 minutes until the whole mixture goes a darker shade of brown. Add the turmeric, the chillies and the chicken.

3. Stir vigorously for 5 minutes, frying the chicken on all sides to brown it. Add the yoghurt and leave the chicken to cook over a high heat, stirring regularly to prevent it from sticking to the bottom of the pan. If it does, add a little water and scrape off with a wooden spoon.

4. After 10 minutes, stir in the rice and fry for 1–2 minutes. Then add one-and-a-half times as much hot water as rice and salt to taste, cover with a lid and leave to cook. Once you have done this, don't be tempted to stir the rice because it will go all mushy.

5. When the water has been absorbed and the rice is cooked (after about 20 minutes), the pulao is ready. Serve hot or cold – it's great either way.

3.

NEVER LET YOU DOWN

Classics and favourites for every occasion –
recipes to rely on!

Miss Masala.

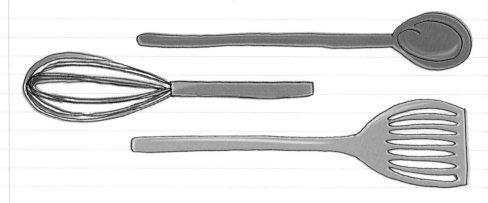

I EMBARKED ON A FEEDING FRENZY. The pint-sized

princess, Bollywood starlet cum international relations student was about to
arrive. Enter my little sister. Fresh from her big-screen foray, featuring wilting
glances and distant stares, the University of Warwick graduate was now in
London for a master's degree.

There was every reason to fuss, I told myself as I ferociously started
chopping onions. She was still recovering from a five-day cabbage soup diet.
Designed to knock off the pounds gained on her last fabulously exotic,
family-funded holiday. Her everyday diet of store-bought Thai green curries,
vegetable stir-fries and salads was hardly enough to nourish a fertile mind.
And why should she suffer a sad life in the big city, without the delights of
home-cooked Indian food?

I set pots and pans on to heat and got to work on two classic recipes from
back home. The family-feeding dichotomy is a tricky one. Relatives are easily
impressed. But also fierce critics. Feeding them calls for simple staples that
they recognise and love. Such as light, fresh meat curries, spicy bhuna
vegetables and subtle pulaos. These recipes are the ones I ache to be back
home for. They feature regularly in our everyday meals. And were the first
ones I experimented with in my early Indian cooking days.

Since then, they have been tried and perfected over the years in my
kitchen. The result: simple classic recipes that delight time and time again.
My only hope is that I can encourage others to cook these recipes for
themselves some day. The ulterior motive behind my labour of love
for the indulged little princess.

Sis walked into the kitchen as I stood bent over two steaming pots, in
spectacles and the customary shower cap. Whistling the theme tune to

Gladiators. 'Oi, freak,' she greeted me, handing over a large box of assorted mithai from the Gupta sweet shop. 'Thanks,' I replied. Inadvertently accepting her gracious compliment along with the treats.

She launched into a monologue about her cute greying tutor, a highly coveted leather bomber jacket and Friday night's drunkenness. I updated her on a big shopping spree, my latest work crisis and the new cocktail lounge of choice. I stirred the food and she cleaned up the mess I was making. We were the A-Team of the home-curry cooking revolution. And as the stories slowed down, I took my chance.

'You know, I'm making Kosha Mangsho for dinner.'

'Wow, I haven't had that since Kol[kata] three months ago!'

'It's really easy to make.' I was sounding scarily like our Diplomatic Service aunty in Birmingham.

Silence.

'I have a super-simple recipe; all you have to do is make sure you have the right ingredients.'

Continued silence.

'I'll be putting it on my blog if you want to look it up later.'

I had turned into the aunty …

I quickly changed the subject to the last call I had made to Mother. Which brought her back to life just in time for dinner. Another knock in my effort to transform her life. Another blow to Miss Masala's fragile ego. On the one hand, my efforts to bring Indian cooking to the lives of ordinary mortals around the world were being wholeheartedly appreciated by almost 20,000 total strangers. On the other, my offers to provide free one-on-one lessons to a totally novice family member were being brutally snubbed.

Never mind, I consoled myself. A master's degree takes one whole year. A year is a long time. I'll just have to keep persevering. Like I did with my own efforts at Indian cooking. The next day, I got a missed call from the hungry student. The free minutes had clearly been exhausted by day three of the new month. The free meal had worn off.

I called her back. 'Yeeeees, what is it?'

'Can you tell me how to make chicken curry?'

My heart skipped a beat. I quietly let out the most almighty scream. Broke into a grin and proceeded to give her a step-by-step breakdown of Murgh Masala, the simplest chicken curry recipe. 'It'll taste just like at home,' I sealed the deal. 'A recipe you can always rely on.'

Murgh Masala
The ultimate simple chicken curry

To successfully complete a degree in England I needed three things, according to my elderly relatives: a firm focus on textbooks, thermal underwear and a basic chicken curry recipe. Chicken curry is quite simply the how-to-boil-an-egg equivalent for any meat-eating Indian girl leaving home. And it was the first Indian dish, along with a Tadka Dal (see page 55), that I was taught to cook.

Every home in India has its own version of chicken curry. The key here is to use only chicken on the bone to enjoy the full flavour of spiced stock in the curry. Once you've cracked the basic recipe you can dress it up for guests, worthy blokes and family members (see variations on page 82).

Feeds 4
1 large onion
2 medium tomatoes
4 garlic cloves
1cm (½in) root ginger
2 tbsp oil
1 pinch of granulated sugar
1 tsp chilli powder
½ tsp turmeric powder
2 tbsp natural Greek yoghurt
6 skinless chicken thighs
   and drumsticks
1 tsp garam masala
1 handful of fresh coriander,
   roughly chopped
salt

1. Peel and finely chop the onion and cut the tomatoes into little bits. Peel and finely chop the garlic and ginger or purée using a hand blender. Pour the oil into a large pan set over a high heat.

2. When the oil is hot, add the pinch of sugar. This will caramelise and give the curry a lovely red glow later without the need for food colouring (see the box on page 84). As the sugar caramelises, stir in the onion and fry for 5 minutes until it starts to brown. Next add the ginger and garlic and stir for a further 5 minutes until the mixture turns golden. Now mix in the tomatoes along with the chilli and turmeric.

3. Fry this masala mixture for at least 5 minutes until the pungent smell gives away to something more subtle. Then lower the heat and simmer, stirring regularly, until you can see oil reappearing through little pores on the surface. This will take 5 minutes or so and you may need to add a bit of hot water to release the spices from the bottom of the pan. »

4. Next, stir in the yoghurt and the chicken pieces. Turn the heat back up high and stir vigorously to seal the chicken on all sides, mixing it well with the other ingredients. When the chicken starts turning white all over, lower the heat to medium, add half a mug of hot water to the pan, cover with a lid and cook for 30 minutes.

5. Remove the lid and cook uncovered for a further 10 minutes to thicken the curry, then stir in the garam masala. Finish by adding salt to taste and serve with lots of chopped fresh coriander sprinkled on top.

THREE WAYS WITH
MURGH MASALA

Add other ingredients to create very different but equally delicious variations. Here are my three top suggestions:

PEPPER CHICKEN CURRY

Leave the yoghurt out. Stir in $\frac{1}{2}$ teaspoon each of freshly ground fennel seeds and black pepper with the other spices. Cook the chicken in its own juices rather than add water.

PALAK (SPINACH) CHICKEN

Marinate 500g (1lb 2oz) of cooked and preferably puréed spinach with the juice of half a lemon when you start cooking. After you've added the sugar to the hot oil, chuck in a bay leaf, a 2.5cm (1in) cinnamon stick, 4 cloves and 4 cardamoms. Add 1 teaspoon each of cumin and coriander powder along with the other spices. Stir the spinach into the cooked chicken at the end and simmer together for 5 minutes to finish.

METHI (FENUGREEK) CHICKEN

Dry-roast 4 cardamoms, 6 black peppercorns, a 2.5cm (1in) cinnamon stick and 1 teaspoon of cumin seeds and grind to a fine powder. Add this to the other spices when cooking. When the masala mixture starts to give off oil, purée it in the pan with a hand blender. Stir in 50g (2oz) of fresh or frozen fenugreek leaves when the chicken is cooked.

Kosha Mangsho
Lamb sautéed in roasted cumin and yoghurt

There are only two things I ask of aunties when they invite me over for home-cooked meals: that they don't ask me to do anything and that they cook Kosha Mangsho for the meal. Kosha Mangsho is the Bengali version of bhuna gosht, a moist stir-fried meat dish without curry.

Traditionally, this is cooked with mustard oil and goat meat. But you can replace them with sunflower oil and good-quality lamb. The trick here is to sauté the lamb really well in the masala mixture, and this is impossible with watery meat. To make this recipe, it is definitely worth that trek to a butcher you can trust.

Feeds 4
2 medium onions
5cm (2in) root ginger
4 garlic cloves
1 tsp cumin seeds
3 tbsp mustard or
  sunflower oil
½ tsp granulated sugar
whole spices
  2 bay leaves
  4 cloves
  4 green cardamoms
  5cm (2in) cinnamon stick
750g (1lb 10oz) diced
  shoulder of lamb
1 tsp chilli powder
1½ tsp turmeric powder
3 tbsp natural Greek yoghurt
salt

1. Peel and finely slice the onions, and peel and finely chop the ginger and garlic or purée them using a hand blender. Dry-roast the cumin under a hot grill for 5 seconds and crush to a powder in a coffee grinder. Pour the oil into a large pan set over a high heat. When it's hot, add the sugar and whole spices.

2. As the spices start to splutter in the hot oil, throw in the onions and fry for 10 minutes until they start turning caramel-coloured. When this happens, add the ginger and garlic and fry for another 5 minutes until the masala mixture turns golden brown.

3. Now, stir in the lamb with the chilli and turmeric. Viciously mix the whole lot until the lamb browns and any water seeping from the meat evaporates. This will take a good 5–10 minutes. Next mix in the yoghurt and add salt to taste. Cover with a lid, lower the heat to medium and leave to cook for 30 minutes.

4. You will need to check the lamb from time to time to make sure it's not getting stuck to the bottom of the pan. If it does, add a little water and scrape the base of the pan with a wooden spoon to release it. After 30 minutes, uncover the pan and cook for a further 20 minutes until the lamb is tender and any liquid has evaporated.

INTRODUCING MUSTARD OIL

This strong-smelling oil with its sharp, nutty taste is often used in Indian cooking and especially in Bengali cuisine. If you want to try it, however, please note that several of the mustard oil brands sold in Indian grocery stores are unfit for consumption. So do check the label before you buy a bottle for cooking. If you were wondering how else it may come in handy, the answer is massage. Mustard oil head and body massages were quite the thing back home.

If you can't find mustard oil, simply substitute with the same quantity of sunflower oil (or any other neutral oil) and add a teaspoon of wholegrain mustard for every tablespoon of oil, mixing it in with any liquid after you've added all the fresh ingredients.

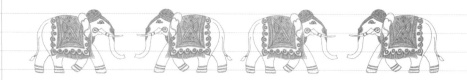

COLOUR ME RIGHT

Ever fancied recreating the DayGlo curries from the local Indian takeaway? Don't. It is far from common to add colour to home-cooked Indian food, with tandoori kebabs being the one exception (see pages 130-1 and 132-3). The rich colours of curry should all be natural, from the herbs, spices and other ingredients. A tiny bit of sugar is sometimes added to hot oil so that it caramelises and gives dishes a red glow.

Baingan Bharta
Smoky roasted aubergine mash

The first time I made this, my husband came running over to tell me I'd set the aubergines on fire. Playing with fire is usually so not my thing. In India I spent Diwali, the festival of lights and firecrackers, hiding under the bed with Gina, the German Shepherd.

Roasting aubergines over a naked flame is about as far as I'll go, but only because of the intense smoky flavour the process imparts to this spicy aubergine mash. If you don't have a gas hob, just roast the aubergines in the oven on a high temperature until they are limp and evenly charred. Then proceed with the rest of the recipe.

Feeds 4
Vegetarian
2 large aubergines
2 medium onions
6 garlic cloves
5cm (2in) root ginger
3 fresh green finger chillies
2 medium tomatoes
15g (½oz) fresh coriander
3–4 tbsp oil
salt

1. If your cooker is a gas one, turn the flame up high on two of the rings. Place an aubergine on each ring to roast. When the skin chars and splits on one side, turn the aubergines over, using tongs, so that they roast evenly. When the aubergines are evenly charred, leave them on a plate to cool.

2. If you don't have a gas hob, you can roast the aubergines in the oven. Preheat the oven to 220°C (425°F), gas mark 7, coat each of the aubergines in 1 teaspoon of oil and roast for 20–25 minutes, turning them halfway through cooking, until softened and evenly browned. Remove from the oven and set aside.

3. While the aubergines are roasting, peel and finely chop the onions, garlic and ginger. Slice the chillies into little pieces, quarter the tomatoes and finely chop the coriander.

4. Next pour the oil into a large pan set over a high heat. When the oil is smoking hot, add the onion, ginger and garlic and fry for 10 minutes until the mixture is pale brown. Then add the chopped tomatoes, coriander and chillies. Fry for a further 5 minutes until the tomatoes disintegrate. 》

5. Lower the heat and, leaving the mixture to gently simmer, peel the roasted aubergines. The skin should just fall off, and where it doesn't, use a sharp knife to tease it away and discard. (This is messy business, by the way.) Add the aubergines to the pan and mash them into the masala mixture. Raise the heat to medium and add salt to taste. With a wooden spoon, keep stirring to make sure there are no lumps of aubergine and that all the ingredients are evenly distributed.

6. Leave to cook for another 10 minutes until a taste test fires up your senses. This spicy recipe is great served alongside toasted pitta bread and a green salad.

Taheri

Healthy vegetable pulao

This north Indian pulao is a staple back home. I have fond memories of Nani, my overweight grandmother, shuffling around in the kitchen, making an enormous pot of golden-yellow Taheri with love and far too many peas. Which we then promptly fished out and left on our plates, much to her horror.

Now Taheri is classic comfort eating in my home too. I never precook the vegetables that go into it, making it a super-simple healthy meal before an evening out or a quiet night in or as fancy rice dish for parties.

Feeds 2
Vegetarian
1 tbsp oil
3 small new potatoes
1 tsp peeled and chopped root ginger
4 cauliflower florets
½ mug of frozen peas
½ tsp turmeric powder
½ tsp chilli powder
½ tsp cumin powder
½ tsp coriander powder
175g (6oz) basmati rice
salt

1. Pour the oil into a large pan on a high heat. Halve the potatoes. When the oil is hot, stir in the ginger and as it starts to brown, mix in the cauliflower, potato and peas.

2. Stir for 1 minute until the vegetables are sealed all over, and add the spices. Mix viciously for a further 2 minutes to coat all the vegetables with the masala.

3. Place the rice in a sieve and rinse it thoroughly in cold water before pouring it into the masala mixture. Stir the rice well for about 2 minutes, mixing it into the spices, then add one-and-a-half times as much hot water as rice. Add salt to taste and bring to the boil. »

4. When the water starts bubbling, lower the heat, cover with a lid and simmer for about 10 minutes, or until the rice has absorbed all the water and is cooked through.

5. Lovely served with a fresh tomato and onion raita, and lime pickle.

DEFINING 'HOME' IS EASY. I spent my first 18 years in good old

Kolkata. Known for Mother Teresa, the infamous Black Hole and a legion of intellectuals. Also, the intense, sweet, spicy and tangy snacks served by loincloth-wearing vendors on dusty pavements. These street foods are perennial favourites – from the spicy puffed-rice jhalmuri to the potato-stuffed crispy pani puris. I grew up on a cocktail of these, developing an iron constitution that would put Wonder Woman to shame.

Sadly, twelve years in England undid my hard work. Now I arrive at Kolkata's Netaji Subhash Chandra Bose or Dum Dum Airport with a lifetime supply of Pepto-Bismol and head for the queue titled 'foreigners'. A gori in my own country.

The first things I crave when I arrive home are a manicure, a pedicure, street food and shopping for semi-precious jewellery. The last trip was no different. To get me from the beautician to the shops, our driver Jamalda ducked potholes, pedestrians, bullock carts and taxis heading straight towards us. At the traffic lights, a reedy teenager told me a heart-wrenching story about his dying mother. I promptly made a generous donation. And as we drove off, Jamalda announced ruefully: 'It was his only brother yesterday.'

I reached New Market with my pride in tatters. Dressed in Gap skinnies with large Chanel sunglasses for protection from the blatant stares. This giant covered market and shopping landmark dates back to the days of the Raj. In a country where new shopping malls spring up like British Z-list celebrities, this is where I seek refuge from the identikit global high street. The maze of cobbled alleys are filled with higgledy-piggledy shops selling everything from wigs and silk scarves to crystal dessert bowls.

My walk to the jewellery shop attracted undue attention. Before I could say 'sterling silver', I had a train

of hustlers running after me. Their offers to lead the way were interspersed with cries of 'shishter, shishter'. Lead the way? I could teach them a thing or two about bargain hunting in New Market. I'm not your sister, I muttered a few times instead. The horror of being mistaken for one of the many tourist shoppers here …

The experience made me hungry. Across the road from New Market is a famous shack selling rolls – Indian parathas wrapped around a filling of spicy kebabs, onions and green finger chillies doused in lemon juice. I took my place in the queue, waiting patiently as the assembly line of men in vests prepared and dispensed rolls. Just as I edged closer to roll nirvana, a man shoved his way in and placed an order. The cheek! 'Excuse me, there is a queue here,' I blurted out with all the finesse of a Bengali Vicky Pollard.

Nonplussed, the man shuffled to the back of the line, while the others stared at me. 'She speaks Bengali,' someone piped up in amazement as if Paris Hilton had won *Mastermind*. I grabbed my chicken roll and headed home. Where I promptly collapsed with a tummy bug. The next two days I nursed piercing pains amidst non-stop admonitions about the fragile state of my foreign belly. And spent the rest of the holiday eating 'street food' strictly in safe restaurants and homes on hygiene high alert.

Indian street food is easy enough to locate in England, I pacified my bruised self on the flight back to Heathrow. I could go to one of the many superb vegetarian restaurants in Wembley, Southall and Tooting. Take a trip to Birmingham's Soho Road. Or simply make my way to central London's branch of a popular fast-food Indian restaurant.

Within a week of arriving back in London, I was craving the intense, spice-filled taste of India's street grub. Soho it was. The restaurant served grazing platters of Indian street food in a bustling canteen-style restaurant. A sophisticated five-star setting in contrast to the eclectic delights of Kolkata's covered market. I popped over after a few drinks in a Carnaby Street pub. Got ushered to a table within a few minutes of queuing. Placed an order and eagerly awaited the Pav Bhaji, Aloo Tikkis and Bhelpuri to appear, while sipping Pinot Grigio with friends. The delicious food arrived on little stainless steel plates. No shoving, no shouting, no staring.

No fun.

Some things are worth risking a gastric implosion. Or, at the very least, meticulously recreating at home. I made for Tooting to buy savoury biscuits and get going.

WHAT TO EAT
ON THE STREET

IF YOUR TUMMY ALLOWS, CHECK OUT THESE STREET FOODS ON A TRIP
TO INDIA, OR IN THE UK IF YOU DON'T MAKE IT THAT FAR:

PANI PURI

Also known as gol gappas and puchkas, these are hollow round
crisps (puris) stuffed with a spiced potato and black chickpea
mash. Dunk them in seriously hot and tangy water (pani) before
shoving the whole lot into your mouth.

JHALMURI AND BHELPURI

Hot and sweet puffed rice mixed with spices, nuts, potato cubes
and crunchy flour noodles. Jhalmuri is the dry and savoury
version, while bhelpuri is topped with crushed biscuits
and whisked with a sweet tamarind sauce.

CHAAT

A mixture of potato pieces and savoury biscuits doused with
yoghurt, spicy chutney, a sweet tamarind sauce and tangy hot
spices. There are several versions and they are all superb.
The aloo chaat (potato), papri chaat (savoury biscuit) and
dahi puri (pani puri served as chaat) are always worth
getting a tummy bug for as far as I'm concerned.
(See also Aloo Channa Chaat on page 95.)

ABOVE Taheri (page 86)

ABOVE Pakoras (page 100)
ABOVE RIGHT Murgh Masala (page 80)

Pav Bhaji
Tangy vegetable curry served with buttered bread rolls

Originally from the west of the country, this is Indian fast food at its finest. A thick vegetable curry (bhaji) is cooked in the centre of a giant sizzling tawa. Hot bread rolls (pav, pronounced 'pao' and meaning 'bread') sit on the edge of the pan. These are then buttered and served with the curry at stations, beaches, parks and shopping centres.

It tastes as good as it looks, as well as being a clever way of using up leftover vegetables. For this recipe, I buy ready-made rolls and purchase Pav Bhaji masala from a spice shop. To make the masala from scratch would mean no less than 20 ingredients, at least ten of which would then languish unused in my cupboard. Thankfully, the masala isn't too potent, so I don't have to worry about my apartment smelling like Chowpatty Beach in Mumbai.

Feeds 4

Vegetarian
1 large carrot
2 medium potatoes
2 medium tomatoes
15–20 green beans
2 medium onions
1cm (½in) root ginger
2 garlic cloves
2 tbsp oil
3 tsp Pav Bhaji masala
1 handful of frozen peas
4 tsp butter
4 white rolls or baps
salt
4 lemon wedges, to serve
1 handful of fresh coriander, roughly chopped, to serve

1. Peel the carrot, potatoes and tomatoes and chop them into small bite-sized pieces. Top and tail the green beans and slice into 1cm (½in) lengths. Peel and finely chop the onions and the ginger and garlic.

2. Pour the oil into a large frying pan set over a high heat. When the oil is sizzling, fry one of the onions and the ginger and garlic over a high heat for 10 minutes until browned. Chuck in the potatoes, carrot and tomatoes and stir for 1 minute.

3. Next add the Pav Bhaji masala and enough hot water to submerge the vegetables. Cover with a lid and cook for 5 minutes until the potatoes are translucent at the edges but not yet cooked through.

4. Add the beans and peas, mixing them well with the other ingredients. Cover again with the lid and keep cooking until the potatoes fall apart when probed with a fork. Add salt to taste and roughly mash the vegetables in the pan. The bhaji should be moist and thick. »

5. Now prepare the pav, or bread. Melt the butter in another frying pan or tawa, set over a medium heat. Heat the grill to high, cut the rolls or baps in half and toast lightly on the inside. Spread each half with the melted butter.

6. Serve the bhaji hot with the buttered rolls and lemon wedges, plus a sprinkling of fresh coriander and the remaining onion.

Chicken Kathi Rolls
Chicken kebab paratha wraps with lemon and chilli

On busy weekdays, a substandard panini is about as exotic as it gets at the local sandwich shop. The toaster doesn't quite melt the cheese. The microwave makes the whole lot soggy. I munch it over the keyboard with a quick diversion on personal e-mails.

I would kill for a Chicken Kathi Roll instead. A juicy kebab smothered in green finger chillies, onions and lemon juice, all wrapped in a hot parathas doused in green chillies, onions and lemon juice. The stuff I grew up eating from bustling roadside food shacks in Kolkata. Sadly, I still haven't found a decent chicken-roll seller in England. This classic delicacy warrants a trip back or a bit of elbow grease in the kitchen.

Feeds 4

4 skinless chicken
    thigh fillets
6 fresh green finger chillies
1cm (½in) root ginger
4 garlic cloves
8 sprigs of fresh coriander
2 lemons
½ tsp turmeric
1 tsp oil
½ tsp garam masala
1 medium onion
4 frozen parathas
salt

1. Cut each chicken thigh into six bite-sized pieces. Chop one of the chillies in half, reserving the half chilli for chopping and adding to the parathas later. Peel and slice the ginger and garlic and, using a hand blender, purée together with the chillies, coriander and the juice of 1 lemon and add salt to taste.

2. Place the chicken pieces in a large bowl and smother with this marinade, along with the turmeric, oil and garam masala. Then leave to sit for at least an hour. (The chicken could be chilled in the fridge overnight.) »

3. When you are ready to eat, preheat the oven to 200°C (400°F), gas mark 6 and line a baking tray with foil.

4. Place the chicken pieces on the tray and bake for 10 minutes, turning over halfway through cooking to bake for a further 10 minutes. In the meantime, peel and finely slice the onion and cook the parathas following the instructions on the packet.

5. Divide the cooked chicken into four and place a portion in a line along the middle of one paratha. Cover with some sliced onion and reserved chopped green finger chilli and drizzle with the juice from the remaining lemon. Wrap up each paratha by rolling up one end to hold the stuffing and then tucking the two sides over like a wrap top. Serve hot with green chutney and chilli sauce for added impact.

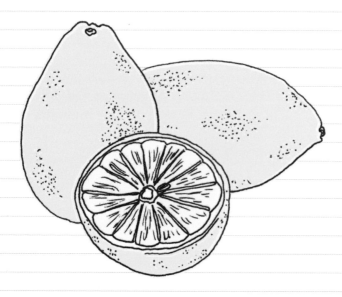

Aloo Channa Chaat
Spicy tangy potato and chickpea platter

Chaats are a serious explosion on the senses – spicy, sour and sweet. For those who have grown up eating delicately flavoured meals, these are the food equivalent of a hard kick on the bottom. Constitutionally incapable of digesting the real deal on the streets at home, I get my fix in fast food cafés and in my great-aunt's colonial marble dining room in Kolkata.

The average chaat needs a handful of specialist ingredients, like a sprinkling of shredded sev or bhujia (crispy deep-fried fritters) or crushed papri (savoury biscuits). But this snack is one I can easily make at home. It requires a simple assembly job with ingredients that can be sourced easily, including that old favourite – tinned chickpeas.

Feeds 4

Vegetarian
4 large potatoes
1 x 400g can of chickpeas
1 x 500g tub of low-fat
  natural yoghurt
1 tsp cumin seeds
½ tsp chilli powder
2 tsp tamarind chutney
  (see page 121)
3 tsp coriander chutney
  (see pages 120–1)
2 tbsp Bombay mix or 'sev'
1 tsp kala namak
  (black rock salt)

1. Peel and chop the potatoes into little pieces. Place in a single layer in a microwave-safe dish, add 5 tablespoons of water, cover with cling film and cook on high for 5–7 minutes, or until softened but still firm. Alternatively, place in a pan of water and boil for 10 minutes on the hob. Drain and allow to cool.

2. In the meantime, rinse the chickpeas well and give the yoghurt a good stir. In a shallow bowl, layer the potatoes first and arrange the chickpeas on top. Spoon over the yoghurt and sprinkle with the spices. Then evenly spread the two chutneys over the top. Finish with a sprinkling of Bombay mix or serve and enjoy as a light snack or a novelty side dish.

TIP FOR CHAAT

While you can buy ready-mixed chaat masala in the shops, chances are you'll have most of the ingredients in it in your cupboard already. This way you can use the individual spices in other recipes too.

KOLKATA GAVE ME THREE of my basic personality traits – an
uncontrollable motor mouth, an intense hatred of housework and a real
love of food.

I was shooting my mouth off in our all-white, chrome, leather and glass
pad in Oval. It was the end of the world as I knew it. The cleaner had staged
a no-show. The flat resembled the interior of a recycling plant. I was
desperately trying to return the contents of my shoe cupboard to its rightful
place. Clothes were lying in mounds around the bedroom floor where they
had been discarded in favour of new ensembles. The contents of my makeup
treasure chest were splayed over the top of the bedside table.

How the mighty have fallen, I sighed to myself, as I rescued a kohl pencil
from my shoe boots. It was almost time to meet a fellow Bengali at the
British Museum. I raced past the fruit and vegetable shop, dry-cleaner and
deli, nodding sweetly to cries of 'yerralrightlove'. I had the London
Underground to look forward to next. Where I would no doubt stand under
someone's armpit with another's frizzy mop in my face.

Life in London is a far cry from the gilt-edged wonderland I grew up in.
Kolkata was a comfortable place indeed. Private car transport. No household
chores. People to rely on. And
to cook your meals. Fond
memories fading fast with
every jolting train stop.

I arrived at the British Museum just
in time for the panel discussion. The
museum was hosting a Bengali food
evening. I was intrigued by the views
of the speakers – a prominent Indian
editor-in-chief, an Indophile BBC
journalist, a fierce London
restaurant critic and her friend,
a leading restaurateur. The Indian
editor-in-chief was the only living
breathing Bengali among them.

The talk was interesting enough. But I
couldn't wait to get a word in. My long-suffering friend
coughed nervously as they opened the floor for questions. *Please don't*

embarrass me, she implored silently with tilted face, slitted eyes and an elbow in my ribs. *Would I ever!* I glared back and sprung my hand up to the ceiling.

I wanted to know what uniquely distinguished Bengali food from other types of regional Indian cuisine. Of course, I already knew the answer to this. Bengalis are famous fish eaters. They cook primarily in mustard oil, use more ginger than garlic and are partial to a bit of sugar even in savoury dishes. The food is typically light and watery, unless of course we're talking celebratory specials. Smug in my authentic knowledge, I eagerly awaited the edification of my less fortunate fellow listeners.

The mic got passed to a panellist. This was a stupid question, he responded sharply. It was like trying to define British food to an alien. It's not possible to express in a nutshell the characteristics of a varied cuisine. Really? A quick summary of bangers and mash, roast dinners and chicken tikka masala would do pretty well, I thought. Before I could retort, however, a wave of protest swelled through the intellectuals peppering the audience. They proceeded to verbally pummel the seated expert, forcing him to acknowledge the special characteristics of Bengali food.

Look what you've done! My friend stared at me disbelievingly. By now, I was beyond caring. We were edging closer towards the grand finale – the cocktail reception. A feast of snacks created by a top Indian chef was about to be served with alcoholic accompaniment. We needed to get from our seats at the back of the auditorium to a strategic spot by the kitchen in 30 seconds flat.

The food was pure genius in little parcels, squares and morsels. What we call samosas, tikkas, patties, bondas and cutlets. These are traditionally served as snacks in between meals or at parties and are seriously moreish. Although cooking a large pot of curry that will fill me for two days seems worth the effort, preparing a snack when I fancy a little something is more questionable in terms of time well spent. It's when I miss the luxury of my Indian home the most.

I do, however, have a handful of recipes that don't need hours of focused attention or deep-frying. Clever classics that never let me down.

SPOTTING AN AUTHENTIC
INDIAN RESTAURANT

Authentic Indian restaurants are slowly but surely growing
in number across the country. To separate the Skodas from the
SLKs of Indian dining, here is what I look out for:

ELDERLY INDIANS
Forget incense and handloom cotton; elderly Indians are the
best indicator of a good-quality Indian restaurant. They cook
rocking Indian food at home and would never be seen dead in
a bolthole that doesn't make curry better than they do,
in the traditional style they know best.

NO BALTI ON THE MENU
No self-respecting Indian would dish out bucket curry.
It doesn't exist in India. Which means it's not authentically
Indian. Which, in turn, means the establishment serving
it is not the real thing.

MEAT ON THE BONE
The best way to cook curry, for maximum flavour,
is by using meat on the bone. Although, sadly, many
authentic establishments have turned to boneless
meat because it cooks more quickly.

Cheese Bondas
Chilli cheese and bread bites

Every now and again, I'll set aside the frivolities of life and consider something truly worth the brain power. Like food wastage. For all my grand ideas of making shopping lists, researching recipes and planning meals, I still fling open the fridge to find the odd soon-to-go-green ingredient that I'd totally overlooked.

Cheese bondas or croquettes are a great way of using up stale bread and odds and ends of hard cheese. As I prefer wholemeal seeded bread, the white stuff purchased for fussy guests and special recipes tends to get forgotten in the fridge. These shallow-fried, addictive bites are not low fat. But who cares when you're saving the world by default?

Makes 8 bondas
Vegetarian
10 slices white bread
1 small onion
3 fresh green finger chillies
100g (3½oz) medium
  Cheddar cheese
2 tbsp plain flour
1 egg
6 tbsp oil
salt

1. Slice the crusts off the bread, peel and finely chop the onion and cut the chillies into little pieces. Grate the cheese into a large mixing bowl, then add the bread, chillies, onion and a little salt to taste.

2. Wet your hands well and squeeze the mixture together until you have a smooth and hard dough. Shape into a large sausage and break into eight equal pieces. With your damp hands, roll each piece into the shape of large cocktail sausage and set aside on a plate.

3. Add the flour to another plate and beat the egg in a small bowl. Then pour the oil into a large frying pan set over a high heat.

4. Finally, roll each bonda in the flour, dip evenly in the egg and fry all eight in two batches until golden brown all over. Eat hot, hot, hot with a dollop of tomato ketchup.

Pakoras
The real onion bhajis

It took me some time to figure out that the greasy, stodgy and murky-coloured objects called 'onion bhajis' in England were what I knew as 'pakoras' back home. Pakoras are a completely different proposition: light, golden yellow and crispy and best eaten piping hot and über-fresh. Whoever started the trend of selling these cold and soggy like sandwiches has a lot to answer for!

Not everything can be perfect, however. Pakoras are usually deep-fried. That's a lot of oil. And they go against rule number one in my kitchen – no deep-frying at home because it's far too fatty. So I shallow-fry pakoras instead, which means a flatter shape than normal but a lower guilt rating for when I fancy these popular snacks.

Makes 4 bhajis
Vegetarian
2 medium onions
100g (3½oz) besan or gram (chickpea) flour
½ tsp baking powder
½ tsp chilli powder
½ tsp cumin powder
8 tbsp oil
salt

1. Peel and finely slice the onions. Sift the flour into a large mixing bowl and add all the powdered ingredients and salt to taste.

2. Spoon in 20 tablespoons of warm water, one at a time, and stir the flour vigorously until you get a thick batter, the consistency of a fruit yoghurt. Now go in with a whisk and beat the batter until large bubbles appear on the surface. Break any lumps by pressing them against the sides of the bowl.

3. Stir the onions into the batter, then pour the oil into a large frying pan set over a high heat. When it starts to sizzle, and using your hand or a wooden spoon, lift a small handful of the battered onions and drop them into the oil. Repeat until there isn't any space left in the pan.

4. Fry each pakora for a few seconds on one side, before flipping over for a few seconds on the other. Remove the pakoras with a slotted spoon and drain on kitchen paper to get rid of any excess oil.

5 Serve immediately with 2 tablespoons of tomato ketchup spiked with ½ teaspoon of chilli powder.

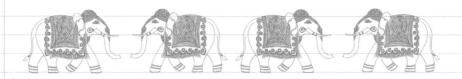

FOR MANY YEARS IT NEVER OCCURRED TO ME to make a roti

(chappati) from scratch. These wholewheat flatbreads are best enjoyed piping hot and soft, cooked and delivered to the dining table by someone else – a cook, your mother or, if you're a lucky man, a good Indian wife. My husband croaked, 'I married the wrong Indian woman' when he saw this in action at a friend's house.

I am more likely to throw a frozen roti at him than painstakingly knead, roll, pan-cook and serve up a fresh one. Don't get me wrong – rotis are really easy to make. They just need more effort to knock up than rice and are easily available in ready-to-cook frozen packs.

I couldn't avoid it forever, though. One fine Saturday morning, I decided to bite the bullet and teach myself how to make rotis. Shamefully, I didn't at the time possess the tawa that is used to dry-roast these. But thankfully, I did have a rolling pin tucked away somewhere. Last used for mixing mojitos at our Cuban-themed house party.

I bought a sack of atta, or chappati flour, in Tooting. This is basically just plain ol' wholewheat flour. The super-sized sacks are clearly aimed at the aforementioned doting wives with luckier husbands than mine. I was convinced I would take to flatbread making like supermodels to celery. That is, once I got started.

As I got stuck into kneading the flour, three thoughts came to my mind:
>> What have I done to my freshly manicured fingernails?
>> There is flour everywhere.
>> I'm a loser if these don't shape into perfect rounds and puff up.

Pleasantly surprised with the shape of my first few rotis, I started screaming, 'Check me out, check me out!' to my bemused hubby. As he left the house to play tennis with a friend, I insisted they both came back for a lunch of fresh rotis and pork vindaloo. I was confident of the future success of my fledgling efforts. I rolled out all the rotis, ready to cook them on their return.

Big mistake.

The rotis came out hard as rocks and flat as pancakes. Hubby and friend ate in silence.

But I remained unfazed. Practice makes perfect, right? With over a kilo of atta left over, Attempt Number Two couldn't be far behind. I spent Sunday making urgent telephone calls to India.

I asked my mother what could have possibly gone wrong. She said: 'It's all in the kneading.' Read: 'I don't have a clue either.' I contemplated calling Dad (what would he know about roti making?), my gran and my great-aunty (it's been a long time since either of them rolled a roti). Desperate, I started thinking of old friends who might know better. The Kolkata primary school teacher (slim chance), the Mumbai film producer (as if) and the Wall Street business analyst (I had finally lost my marbles).

Monday arrived and I was none the wiser. The week started with a very English business breakfast meeting followed by shockingly hard work on three-inch red stilettos. But I just couldn't stop thinking about soft, fluffy rotis. Back home, I fired up the MacBook. And help was at hand where I least expected it. In the two days since my online roti-making rant, the blogosphere had rallied to my rescue. Wise blogger buddies and experienced readers had left useful nuggets of advice on the site for me.

I poured myself two double vodka cranberries. Calm and in control as you can be only after two stiff drinks, I took to roti making with renewed gusto. The results were not bad at all. Soft and fluffy. Almost round. Two out of three filled up with air. That's near perfect in my books! The straightforward way to crack a classic after a long hard day at work.

MY FAVOURITE FLATBREADS

What wouldn't I give to have our cook Dada in London, lovingly rolling and serving piping hot flatbreads? If I can't find the time to make them at home, I have to be content eating these at restaurants, weddings and other special occasions. Lately, my local supermarket has started stocking frozen ready-to-cook flatbreads. They're quite fatty, but a wonderful change from plain rice and pulaos.

THESE ARE MY FAVOURITE FLATBREADS, IN NO PARTICULAR ORDER:

ROTIS

Also called chappatis, these are made with wholewheat flour and roasted without oil on a tawa and then cooked over a naked flame until soft and puffed up.

PARATHAS

Made with plain flour, these are lightly shallow-fried in oil. They have a crispier texture than rotis. You can also make them with wholewheat flour and stuff them with vegetables for a simple meal.

NAAN

While this is also made with plain flour, the dough uses yeast and is kneaded with yoghurt and milk. Naan is traditionally cooked quickly in a tandoor oven, where the pliable dough rises and forms little dark spots. As well as the popular nutty Peshawari Naan (see pages 168-9), I adore naan stuffed with keema. A real treat!

LUCHI

These are swollen deep-fried pancakes. Usually made with plain flour, they can also be made with wholewheat flour and are traditionally served with stir-fried or curried potatoes. One reserved for Indian holidays only, I'm afraid.

Rotis

Traditional everyday wholewheat flatbreads

Buying a sack of atta was the best motivation I needed to perfect roti making. For every opportunity I gave up to make a batch, I had to sacrifice space for other store-cupboard essentials, needed for our Italian, Chinese, Japanese and classic British home-cooked meals.

It has been well worth the effort, though. Rotis are at their best dunked into thick, wholesome dal or used to scoop up tender lamb curry. I wouldn't start making them on a daily basis just yet. But when I'm reheating leftovers for dinner, homemade rotis are just what the doctor orders to complete the meal.

Makes 4
Vegetarian
110g (4oz) wholewheat flour or atta (chappati flour), plus extra for dusting
1 pinch of salt
4 tsp butter

1. Place the flour and salt in a large mixing bowl. Add 1 tablespoon of hot water and mix it vigorously into the flour. You will get a crumbly mixture. Add a bit more hot water and repeat the process. The idea is to break the flour down and incorporate plenty of air into the dough.

2. Keep adding water (about half a mug in total) until you get a hard dough that does not stick to your fingers. You won't need all the hot water in the cup. Now go into the dough with your knuckles, kneading viciously. I did this about six times and got bored, but the more you do this, the softer the rotis will be.

3. Roll the dough into a thick sausage and break it off into four parts, forming each of these into a dough ball. Leave the dough balls in the mixing bowl, cover with a clean damp cloth or tea towel and allow to rest for 30 minutes.

4. After the dough balls have rested, lightly flour a chopping board and set a large, non-stick frying pan or tawa over a medium heat. Dip the first dough ball in the flour, flatten and roll it out into a disc about 1mm thick. If you don't get a perfectly round shape, just use your hands to stretch the roti out in the wonky places. »

5. Now place the roti in the frying pan or tawa and heat for 2 minutes on each side until little bubbles appear on the side being cooked. You may need to press down on to the roti with a slotted spatula to encourage this.

6. When the bubbles appear, take the frying pan or tawa off the heat and toast the roti directly on the hob (gas or electric) for a couple of seconds on each side, until it swells up. Don't worry if it burns a little; this will just add to the smoky flavour. Use tongs (ice bucket ones will do nicely) to flip it over, unless you have asbestos fingers.

7. When the pale brown spots on the roti turn darker and it swells up, that means it's done. Remove from the heat and keep warm in a parcel of kitchen foil or a clean tea cloth. Then start the process all over again with the remaining dough balls. Serve the rotis hot, lightly buttered on one side.

TIP

Before you start making naan or rotis, line the work surface and floor area where you'll be standing with newspaper. That way you can simply dispose of the floury newspaper rather than having to mop up the mess.

Naan

Soft oven-fresh homemade tandoori bread

The first time I made naan, the dough clung to my powder-pink-painted fingernails like Elasto Girl. I prised it off with a butter knife and lashings of plain flour. Then the whole lot doubled into this enormous, heaving pile of dough that no amount of kneading could rescue. So I rolled the dough in some more flour. The whole lot contracted. Which made my earlier addition of yeast totally pointless. At which point I stormed out of my kitchen, swearing like an Indian fishwife.

I'm happy to report that, a few trials later, I have taken to naan-making like a WAG to It Bag shopping. The best thing about naan is that you can make loads in one go, reheat some for guests and freeze several for later.

Makes 6

Vegetarian
300g (11oz) plain flour,
  plus extra for dusting
7g sachet fast-action yeast
½ tsp salt
1 tbsp nigella seeds
6 tbsp low-fat natural
  yoghurt
6 tbsp whole milk
2 tbsp oil
25g (1oz) butter

1. Sift the flour into a large mixing bowl and add the yeast, salt and nigella seeds. Mix the yoghurt and milk together and warm in a microwave on high for about 40 seconds. Alternatively, heat in a small pan on the hob until warmed through.

2. Pouring in the yoghurt and milk a little at a time, mix with the flour until you get a soft and pliable dough that doesn't stick to your fingers. If you add too much liquid, just chuck in a bit more flour to get the desired consistency.

3. Knead the dough well, punching it with your knuckles and rolling it backwards and forwards until you are bored or tired. Five minutes is my limit, but the longer you can keep going – up to 10 minutes – the better the outcome.

4. Next, tip the dough ball on its side, coat the bowl with the oil and place the dough back in the centre. Now cover the bowl with a clean damp cloth and leave the dough to sit in a warm place for 2 hours. On a cold day, I usually turn the oven on to its lowest setting and leave the dough in there. »

5. After 2 hours, the dough will be very frothy and will have doubled in size. Punch it again until it shrinks, re-cover with the cloth and return it to its warm place to sit for another hour.

6. When the time is up, take the dough out and punch it down again. Preheat the oven to its highest setting, placing a baking tray lined with foil on the middle shelf.

7. Finally, tear the dough into six equal portions. Dust a rolling pin and a chopping board with flour and roll out each piece of dough to roughly 5mm (¼in) thick, then stretch it by hand into a teardrop shape. Try not to use too much flour at this stage, as it'll make the naans crisp when cooked. Professionals just stretch the dough out with their hands rather than using a rolling pin.

8. Place two naans on the foil-lined baking tray and bake for 3–4 minutes on one side only until brown spots appear and they begin to swell up in places. Brush with melted butter and leave to sit wrapped in a clean warm cloth or foil. Repeat the process with the rest of the dough until your 6 naans are ready.

9. Serve immediately or dampen lightly with water and heat in a microwave for 30 seconds each or in a medium–hot oven for 5 minutes when you are ready to feast.

INTRODUCING NIGELLA SEEDS

Nigella seeds (kala jeera) are also known as black onion or black cumin seeds. These are small and dark with a distinctive sharp and peppery taste.

4.

LIGHT AND BRIGHT

Light lunches and food for warmer days

Miss Masala.

INNER-CITY SUMMER. WHAT AN ADVENTURE.

The BBC weather page finally decided on sunny and hot. It was time to extract the little shift dress, patent leather sandals and celebrate. I started the day squashed on a sweltering Underground train deemed unfit by the EU for cattle transportation. Then made it into the office just in time for the big Arctic freeze. The office air conditioning had been readjusted to recreate midwinter. Who cares if it is 30°C and baking outside? We PR people would rather freeze our tits off than perspire.

The bright blue sky was barely visible through the skylight. But it was having a remarkably mood-lifting effect on everyone. Helped by the Friday morning feeling. The morning flew by with no swearing at the printer. No verbal outbursts at the computers. By elevenses, we had started plotting the lunchtime escape – al fresco salads at the local gastropub. The mood turned feverish with expectation by midday. By lunchtime, there was no stopping us. Half the team was dispatched to find a sunny sheltered spot while the rest of us followed close behind.

Except the other 10,000 offices in the area had had the same brilliant idea.

The smart gastropub was heaving with local office workers. Inside was packed to capacity with linen trousers, warm beers and potato wedges. The staff could barely focus as they rushed around serving lunchtime burgers and salads. Outside, the scene was even more chaotic. Customers had spilled out of the pub's tiny patio area and on to the pavement. There were people everywhere I looked.

Deflected but not defeated, we propped ourselves against a brick wall. Handbags and other items were deposited on the ground in one big heap. A liquid lunch it was to be, then. All eyes turned to the most senior member of the team – a Kensington-based Welshman. His credit card was going to deliver the summer lunchtime extravaganza we were all hoping for. He tried to fake a last-minute client meeting. But it was too late. I marched the grudging MD to the bar. The power of my lip-gloss was going to be put to the test in the most challenging circumstances.

Ten minutes of pouting around the bar and the Welshman finally had a cute male bartender's attention. I quickly placed the order.

'We'll have three jugs of Pimm's, please.'

'We've run out of ice and mint.'

What? You might as well throw the Pimm's out, I thought quietly.

'In that case, we'll have three bottles of the Sauvignon Blanc.'

'They'll be at room temperature, I'm afraid – we've just restocked the fridge.'

What's the point of a pub in summer without mint, ice and cold Sauvignon Blanc?

I didn't fancy white wine posing as donkey's piss. We collectively identified a relatively cool Pinot Grigio and made it back outside, where the sunshine had gone a little hazy. Just like our previously boundless enthusiasm. I had the weekend to look forward to next. When I would share the city's green spots with London's 7.5 million inhabitants and feral pigeon population.

Summer for me is all about little dresses, big heat and fresh urban living. Also volatile tempers and limited patience. This is not the time for rich, spicy dishes smothered in a thick curry of tomato, onion or coconut milk. This is the time of the year for light brunches and dinners that fill you up without weighing you down. Easy dishes that can be paired with simple shop-bought essentials.

These summer specials work in the great outdoors, cooler indoors or whenever you fancy a lighter touch.

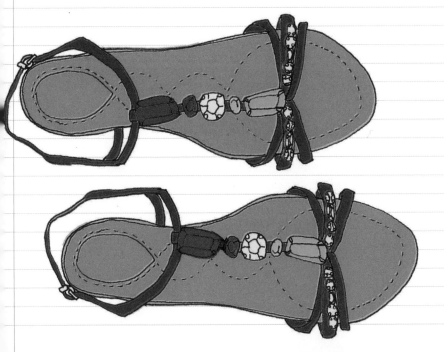

Aloo Chenchki
Potatoes and onions sautéed with nigella seeds

The British potato season may begin in April, but spuds are my all-year all-rounder. I love potatoes, especially in the guise of evil fatty fries alongside a gin and tonic in a pub or bar. One bite into that crunchy exterior and soft, starchy inside and all thoughts of zero-size clothing and healthy eating are instantly banished.

At home is where I regulate potato eating. Evenings are a mealtime no-go for potatoes and when I do make them I try not to precook them, so that all their goodness is preserved. This recipe is a summer potato sauté. It's light, fresh and equally good whether stuffed into pitta bread, served with rice and dal, or as something a bit different to go with grilled steak.

Feeds 4
Vegetarian
2 medium potatoes
1 large onion
1 tbsp oil
1 tsp nigella seeds
2 fresh green finger chillies
salt

1. Peel and slice the potatoes into 1cm (½in) thick discs and then into 1cm (½in) wide chips. Peel and halve the onion widthways and cut into thick rings.

2. Pour the oil into a large frying pan set over a high heat. When it's hot, add the nigella seeds and as they start to sizzle, stir in the onions and potatoes. Cover with a lid and sauté for 5–10 minutes, removing the lid every now and then to stir the mixture, until the potatoes are translucent.

3. Slit the green finger chillies and stir them in, add salt to taste and continue cooking, uncovered, for a further 5 minutes until the potatoes are soft to the touch. They should be cooked through but still retain their shape.

Paneer Bhujia

Paneer scrambled with tomatoes, onion and fresh coriander

You know that feeling? When you've enjoyed one glass too many of an ice-cold drink in warm weather. It's late. You're famished. But not bleary-eyed enough to crawl into the local takeaway. For me, this is when a decent, healthy meal needs to be cooked in record time before things take an ugly turn.

Paneer Bhujia is a dead-simple scrambled dish made with quality summer ingredients – juicy red tomatoes and highly addictive fresh coriander. I ate this back in India with ready-made parathas and some pickle. But you could just as easily spoon it over a thick slice of toast as a more exotic alternative to scrambled eggs.

Feeds 2

Vegetarian
1 small onion
2 small tomatoes
250g (9oz) paneer
2 tbsp oil
1 tsp cumin seeds
1 large bay leaf
¼ tsp turmeric powder
½ tsp chilli powder
4–5 sprigs of fresh coriander
salt

1. Peel and roughly chop the onion, then roughly chop the tomatoes and the paneer.

2. Pour the oil into a small pan set over a high high. When the oil is hot, add the cumin seeds and bay leaf. As they sizzle up, stir in the onions and tomatoes.

3. Stir-fry for about 5 minutes until the onions have softened but not browned and the tomatoes have disintegrated. Now mix in the turmeric and chilli and fry for a further 2 minutes until the pungent smell of the raw spices has toned down.

4. Finally, add the paneer and mix it in thoroughly, smashing it up with your wooden spoon as you stir, to get a crumbly mixture. Mix in salt to taste, add the coriander and eat immediately while the paneer is still soft and juicy.

REFRESHING RAITAS
TO ACCOMPANY
SPICY DISHES

Give me a raita at any time of the year. But summer is when they really come into their own. These side dishes of savoury, delicately flavoured yoghurt are a fresh and cooling antidote to a spicy Indian meal – just what the tummy needs, especially in hot weather.

I make raita with potatoes, boondis (little chickpea flour balls) and even with boiled eggs (see page 159)! But the two that regularly accompany my meals are Cucumber and Mint Raita and Kachumbar Raita. My trick is to use kala namak or black rock salt (available ready powdered) instead of the normal white stuff. Kala namak has a sharp sulphuric edge to it that's divine with plain yoghurt. Trust me!

CUCUMBER AND MINT RAITA
500G (1LB 2OZ) LOW-FAT NATURAL YOGHURT*
250G (9OZ) CUCUMBER
10 LEAVES OF FRESH MINT, FINELY CHOPPED, OR 1 TSP DRIED MINT
1 TSP KALA NAMAK (BLACK ROCK SALT)

Whip the yoghurt with a fork for 1 minute until smooth and
bubbly. Peel and chop the cucumber into tiny little pieces,
then stir into the yoghurt along with the fresh mint (if using).
Pour the mixture into a shallow serving dish. Sprinkle over
the dried mint (if using) and the black salt and refrigerate
until ice cold before tucking in.

KACHUMBAR RAITA
100G (3½OZ) CUCUMBER
1 MEDIUM ONION / 2 MEDIUM TOMATOES
1 TSP CUMIN SEEDS
500G (1LB 2OZ) LOW-FAT NATURAL YOGHURT*
TSP CHILLI POWDER / 1 TSP KALA NAMAK (BLACK ROCK SALT)

Peel the cucumber and onion, halve and deseed the tomatoes
and then chop the three vegetables into the smallest pieces
you can manage. I normally use my mini chopper for this.

Next dry-roast the cumin under a hot grill for 5 seconds,
then crush to a powder in a coffee grinder. Whip the yoghurt
for 1 minute with a fork, stir in the chopped vegetables and
pour the mixture into a shallow serving dish. Sprinkle
over the cumin, chilli powder and black salt and
refrigerate until ice cold.

* If you use thick Greek yoghurt, you'll have a fabulous
dip for nachos or lightly salted crisps.

Bean Salad
Spicy mixed beans with cucumber and tomatoes

Mother arrives in London in the height of summer with a suitcase filled with spices. Years of dragging her around spice shops here, and she's still convinced her supplies are inherently superior. Like her homemade roasted cumin and tea masalas. Which then brew for years in my cupboard until I coldheartedly dispose of them.

    While she's around, she does her best to put them to good use. Mixed bean salad is her speciality and one that has proved invaluable to me. I quickly toss it together for lunch or for when friends drop in to say hi. Recreating her recipe with a tin of mixed kidney, adzuki and cannellini beans (although any combination would do), in addition to the fresh ingredients. This earthy salad is lovely with fish fillets grilled with a fresh herb marinade (see page 60, marinade used for Masala Fish) or as a healthy side dish for a barbecue.

Feeds 2–4
Vegetarian
2 tsp cumin seeds
½ tsp ajwain seeds
juice of 1 lemon
1 x 400g can of mixed beans
1 small onion
½ cucumber
2 medium tomatoes
salt

1. First make the dressing. Preheat the grill to high and dry-roast the cumin seeds for 5 seconds, removing them as soon as you can smell them cooking. Crush in a coffee grinder, then mix in a small bowl with the ajwain seeds, lemon juice and salt to taste. Leave to sit while you prepare the rest of the dish.

2. Rinse and drain the beans and add to a large mixing bowl. Peel and finely chop the onion, cut the cucumber and tomatoes into little pieces and chuck all these into the bowl.

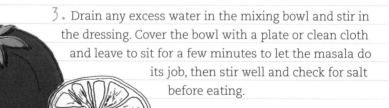

3. Drain any excess water in the mixing bowl and stir in the dressing. Cover the bowl with a plate or clean cloth and leave to sit for a few minutes to let the masala do its job, then stir well and check for salt before eating.

SUMMER ARRIVED. So did my designated Greenfingers Day, when I take my annual stab at gardening. Dressed in my grungiest outfit, I dragged my man to a plant nursery in the suburbs.

We tried to blend into the sea of seasoned gardeners – a few green grannies, several bewellied families and some professional landscape-gardening types. I, meanwhile, walked into thorns. Shrank bank from bugs. Desperately trying to recognise the flora (and avoid the fauna). But I wasn't fooling anyone. Three cries of 'Look honey, passionflower/clematis/ivy', pointing to none of these, and a kindly salesperson walked over with a barely suppressed grin, asking how he could help.

I desperately wanted a creeper. To block out the direct view into our neighbours' kitchen. And to prevent them from witnessing the regular occurrences of sordid drunkenness in ours. Preferably something that grew bushy and tall against a bamboo trellis. Without regular watering, sunlight or attention. Or soil for that matter. We were talking about a potted plant for a three-foot-square, moss-ridden balcony.

A giant vine was clearly out of the question. I settled on a medium hedge and a dwarf jasmine climber. Brought various plants back and got to work on my patch of green. Oversized chrome planters and compost had been duly acquired. Now all I needed was a set of mini garden tools. By this time I'd caught the attention of various neighbours, who promptly came out to watch the spectacle. One lit a cigarette, another discussed her recent exotic holiday, while the wails of someone's toddler mingled with the laughter of the aforementioned trendy record company executive, now inebriated, in the garden below.

It felt like *Eastenders*.

Under pressure to show off my gardening capabilities, I decided to improvise. Aided by a cheese slicer and kitchen scissors, I shoved the hedge into a planter, much to the amusement of my assembled neighbours. I planted some basil, mint and a selection of other plants that I was assured would grow into great big flowering bushes.

The next few weeks were critical. I enthusiastically watered, fed the plants copious amounts of fertiliser and talked to the leaves – especially after several G&Ts.

The unorthodox approach paid off. Within weeks the balcony had transformed into a mini Amazon jungle. In fact, the small pot of mint had turned into a veritable bush! It had banished the basil to a small corner of the planter and started viciously eyeing the thriving Jasmine creeper. I. Needed. Mint. Recipes. And before the dastardly herb audaciously struck my enormous hedge. Cucumber and Mint Raita immediately sprang to mind, as did Haryali Murgh, chicken curry with spinach and mint.

I made an urgent trip to the butcher and the ethnic markets in Tooting. Cooking in the summer calls for the best-quality seasonal ingredients. My favourites are juicy cucumbers, bright red tomatoes and handfuls of fresh herbs. Used in delicately seasoned, light, summery dishes, with no need to be drowned in a sea of spices. Or preserved for the days and weeks to come as pickles, chutneys and preserves to accompany meals.

Hariyali Murgh
Chicken in a light coriander, mint and spinach curry

Apart from fresh mint gluts, recipe inspiration hits me at the most unexpected moments. A night of cocktails and dinner served alongside burlesque, vintage parlour humour and retro orange-peel nudity and I couldn't wait to put some legs and thighs on show myself. Of chicken, that is …

Hariyali Murgh – chicken steeped in a delicate curry of fresh spinach, coriander and mint – is sure to take centre stage. It's easy on the taste buds, sublime in warm weather and just the comfort needed after a late night of mischief.

Feeds 4
6 chicken thighs
 and drumsticks
1cm (½in) root ginger
4 garlic cloves
3 spring onions
1 tbsp oil
1 tsp coriander powder
1 tsp cumin powder
100g (3½oz) fresh spinach
25g (1oz) fresh mint
25g (1oz) fresh coriander
1 fresh green finger chilli
juice of ½ lemon
salt

1. Skin the chicken pieces and purée the ginger and garlic with a tablespoon of water and using a hand blender. Chop up the full length of the spring onions. Pour the oil into a large pan set over a high heat.

2. When the oil starts sizzling, throw in the salad onions and the ginger and garlic purée. Stir the mixture for about 1 minute until the ginger and garlic goes a pale golden brown. Now add the chicken pieces and the coriander and cumin powders and cook for 5 minutes, turning the chicken from time to time to seal the meat all over. »

3. In the meantime, wash and drain the spinach and place in another large pan. Cover with a lid and cook for 3–5 minutes until completely wilted. Alternatively, place in a microwave-safe dish, cover with cling film and cook in a microwave for about 3 minutes on high. Pick the mint leaves from their stems and cut off the thick ends of the coriander stalks.

4. In a blender or food processor, purée the cooked spinach with the mint, coriander, green finger chilli and lemon juice. Pour this fresh green sauce over the chicken, lower the heat to medium, cover with a lid and cook for about 30 minutes.

5. If the chicken becomes dry during this time, add half a mug of hot water to help it cook. When the meat separates from the bone and the curry is moist but not watery, remove from the heat and serve with some steaming hot basmati rice and a contented smile.

INTRODUCING TAMARIND

The sour brown seedpods of the tamarind tree are soaked in warm water, strained and added to dishes to inject a slightly sweet yet tart flavour. It is sold either as a solid bock of seedpods, perfect for chutneys, or as a paste that can be stirred straight into curries and dals with no further preparation.

CHUTNEY VS. PICKLE

What's a good Indian meal without a generous helping of chutney or pickle? The major difference between the two is that chutney is made with fresh ingredients, cooked and eaten straight away. Pickle, on the other hand, is fermented and preserved for several months. Chutneys can accompany dry dishes like tikkas and kebabs. Simply sparkle on their own as dips. And control overzealous plants. These are my all-time favourites:

TAMATAR CHUTNEY

200G (7OZ) RIPE RED TOMATOES / 1CM ($\frac{1}{2}$ IN) ROOT GINGER
1 TBSP OIL / 1 DRIED LONG RED CHILLI
50G (2OZ) GRANULATED SUGAR / 1 TBSP RAISINS

Roughly chop the tomatoes and peel and grate the ginger. Pour the oil into a small frying pan set over a high heat. When it starts sizzling, crumble in the red chilli and add the ginger. Stir-fry for 1 minute until the ginger turns pale golden.
Next add the tomatoes and cook for about 5 minutes until they disintegrate. Add the sugar and raisins and stir for a further 5 minutes until the tomatoes take on a jamlike texture. Remove from the heat, allow to cool and then store in an airtight container in the fridge for up to 5 days.

DHANIYA PUDINA CHUTNEY

125G (4$\frac{1}{2}$OZ) FRESH CORIANDER LEAVES
125G (4$\frac{1}{2}$OZ) FRESH MINT LEAVES / 3 FRESH GREEN FINGER CHILLIES
FRESHLY SQUEEZED JUICE OF 1 LEMON / SALT

Remove the hard stalks from the herbs and chillies and purée all the ingredients in a blender or food processor until you get a smooth and rich green dipping sauce. You could add a tablespoon of natural yoghurt or plain water, if you like, to help with the blending. Store in an airtight container in the fridge and use within a week.

COCONUT CHUTNEY

1 MUG OF GRATED COCONUT (I BUY THE FROZEN STUFF FROM CHINESE GROCERS)
2 FRESH GREEN FINGER CHILLIES / 1 TBSP OIL
1 PINCH OF ASAFOETIDA / 1 TSP MUSTARD SEEDS
4 CURRY LEAVES / 2 DRIED LONG RED CHILLIES / SALT

Purée the coconut and green chillies in a food processor with 2 tablespoons of water until coarse and thick. Pour the oil into a small frying pan set over a high heat. When the oil is hot, add the asafoetida, mustard seeds, curry leaves and red chillies and as they sizzle up, pour them into the coconut paste, stirring to mix. Add salt to taste, place in an airtight container in the fridge and enjoy for up to a week.

TAMARIND CHUTNEY

5CM (2 IN) BALL OF TAMARIND / 2 TSP LIGHT MUSCOVADO SUGAR
$1/2$ TSP FRESHLY GROUND BLACK PEPPER
$1/2$ TSP KALA NAMAK (BLACK ROCK SALT)

Soak the tamarind in 5 tablespoons of boiling water mixed with the sugar, black pepper and salt, and allow to sit for 15 minutes. Strain the tamarind of its juices twice until you get a thick, sweet and sour chutney. Use immediately with vegetable tikkas and shallow-fried snacks. Kept in an airtight container in the fridge, this will last for about five days.

Lamb Korma

Lamb stewed in yoghurt and whole black peppercorns

I have a real issue with curry-house kormas. Sugary and bland, these are a far cry from the aromatic stews I enjoyed with parathas in fancy Indian restaurants back home. Nothing gets my goat more than people saying, 'My favourite Indian dish is korma', when they clearly don't have a clue what a real one tastes like!

Up north they cook korma in a light yoghurt curry, while down south coconut milk is used. My version is a nod to the yoghurt-based version – a simple and flavoursome dish that is easy on the taste buds and the tummy.

Feeds 4

300g (11oz) natural
   Greek yoghurt
3 tbsp oil
whole spices
   4 cardamoms
   4 cloves
   4 whole black peppercorns
   2 small bay leaves
½ tsp granulated sugar
2 large onions
4cm (1½in) root ginger
4 garlic cloves
¾ tsp turmeric powder
¾ tsp chilli powder
750g (1lb 10oz) lamb
   neck fillet
¾ tsp garam masala
salt

1. Pour the oil into a large pan set over a high heat and, when hot, add the whole spices and the sugar. Peel and finely chop the onions. When the sugar caramelises, chuck them into the pan and fry for 10 minutes until translucent.

2. In the meantime, peel and finely chop the ginger and garlic or purée them using a hand blender. Add these to the onions and fry for 5 minutes until the mixture starts going brown. Add the turmeric and chilli powder and fry for 5 minutes until the pungent smell tones down. Then add the yoghurt and fry for a further 5 minutes. The yoghurt may split or curdle at first but will reconstitute while cooking, making no difference to the final taste and texture of the dish.

3. Chop up the lamb into bite-sized chunks and add to the pan, stirring it well into the masala mixture. Brown the meat on all sides and then lower the heat to medium, cover with a lid and cook for 30 minutes. Remove the lid and cook for a further 30 minutes until the lamb is tender when probed with a fork. To finish, stir in the garam masala for the last 5 minutes of cooking and add salt to taste.

Dosakaya Pappu
Light and cooling cucumber dal

When I first started blogging, I quaked at the thought of entering the world of bespectacled geeks with too much time on their hands. I couldn't be more wrong. I discovered a whole new world of gobby, busy food lovers out there that I didn't even know existed. And learnt more about Indian food and in-laws than a lifetime of experience could have taught me.

This cucumber dal was one of the gems I stumbled across. The recipe is from the south-eastern state of Andhra Pradesh. It's traditionally made with Indian cucumbers called dosakai – shaped like melons but small and yellow in colour – but I just substitute them for juicy and widely available green cucumbers for a wholesome summer dal.

Feeds 4
Vegetarian
100g (3½oz) toor
  (split yellow) lentils
½ tsp chilli powder
¼ tsp turmeric powder
½ cucumber
1 tbsp oil
1 pinch of asafoetida
½ tsp mustard seeds
½ tsp cumin seeds
12 curry leaves, fresh
  or frozen
2 dried long red chillies
salt

1. Wash the lentils thoroughly under a cold tap, then place in a medium pan, cover with twice as much water as lentils, add the chilli and turmeric powders and bring to a gentle boil. In the meantime, chop the cucumber into 5cm (2in) chunks. There's no need to peel them.

2. After about 20 minutes, when the lentils start losing shape and integrating with the water, chuck in the cucumber pieces. Then mash two spoonfuls of the lentils on the sides of the pan to thicken the dal. If it becomes too dry and the lentils start to splutter, add half a mug of hot water and keep cooking on a gentle boil.

3. As the dal starts resembling a thick soup, make the tadka. Pour the oil into a small frying pan set over a high heat. When it's hot, add, in order, the asafoetida, the mustard and cumin seeds, curry leaves and chillies, and allow them to sizzle in the hot oil. This should take only seconds, or the seeds will burn to a crisp.

4. Now quickly stir the whole lot into the dal, add salt to taste and serve hot with some plain steamed rice.

I SAT IN FRONT OF THE TELLY, RIVETED. On show was a

very British celebrity chef. Building a tandoor oven in his back garden, which was the size of my local park. Jealous, moi? Not in the slightest. I simmered for a few seconds, toying with the idea of amateur masonry in our communal back garden. Hmmm. Not so great for building health and safety. Perhaps a mini tandoor oven on my kitchen floor? Not so great for glossy black kitchen floor tiles.

Sod it. I had better things to do. Like make my way to a friend's barbecue in another communal garden down the road. Summer barbecues send a tingle of excitement down my spine. All those cheap sausages. Almost-cooked chicken thighs and drumsticks. The cheap wine fished out of ice-cold plastic buckets. And limitless opportunity to show off the fine delights of Indian tandoori cooking. The marinated skewers, cubes and cuts of meat, fish, seafood, paneer and vegetables. Drenched in lemon juice, sprinkled liberally with fresh coriander and sliced onions, and served with spicy green chutney.

I didn't get my act together on time to prepare my contribution. It was just as well. My friend Rosie is the spunky author of the ingeniously titled *Spooning with Rosie* and a Brixton deli-café-running trendy food genius. Only she can bake cupcakes and serve customers while handing out coffees to local crack addicts. She was trialling a mini selection of her cookbook recipes at the barbecue. And there wasn't a cheap sausage in sight. The wooden tables were spilling over with homemade salads, bowls of her lethal punch and fresh platters of barbecued ribs. Sheltered by umbrellas in the pouring rain, we ate, talked and drank as if it was a hot summer's day.

For all this talk of tandoors and gardens, decent weather is clearly the hardest thing to come by. The showery summer had been more Mordor than Marrakech. Still, I had a birthday party to look forward to the following week. Our Australian neighbour upstairs had planned an all-day barbecue to celebrate turning 21 again. He acquired an Outback, the aptly branded barbecue. Downloaded the latest tunes. And invited a motley crew of colleagues, friends and neighbours to the festivities.

We feverishly monitored the weather forecast. And, horror of horrors, the weather decided not to cooperate. The Outback was transported to the three-foot-square balcony of their second-floor flat. Which threw my party trick into total disarray. Sausages and burgers would work just fine on the billowing balcony monster. But tandoori chicken was clearly out of the question unless our neighbours fancied masala bedlinen and curry upholstery.

I took a chance on Seekh Kebabs, juicy ground lamb and herb cutlets on skewers. These famous kebabs are Mughlai, dating back to when the Mughals held sway in India. It was they who gave us the rich, fragrant delicacies that Indian cuisine is famous for – the meat biryanis, creamy dal makhanis and tender kebabs. If anything was going to impress the 30 grown men and women, it was these kebabs.

But by the time I had mixed the lamb, shaped the kebabs, taken a shower and slipped on a ra-ra miniskirt, the party was in full swing. I walked in, handbag in one hand and stainless-steel platter of the stuff in the other. Mounds of food lay all over the table. But the crowd was more interested in the giant Smirnoff on tap than soft, buttery kebabs of venerable Mughal origin.I grabbed a drink, keen to catch up with the rest of the crowd. Before I knew it, the iPod came on. Food was relegated to history, the building shook from dance moves perilously executed on the slippery kitchen floor.

A few hours later, the kebabs remained forgotten. The party was kicking. But my energy levels weren't. I sneaked off quietly, taking the platter of food back downstairs with me. Turned the grill on. Cooked a few to perfection. As the guests launched into a Steps routine upstairs, I breathed a sigh of relief. Cheesy choreographed dance routines meant they wouldn't notice the missing kebabs. I launched into them with a large squirt of tomato ketchup.

The next morning, I woke up relatively fresh but consumed with guilt about the Seekh Kebabs. There were six left over. The sun was shining. The Outback sat on the upstairs balcony amidst fag butts and empty bottles for recycling. I had a vision of the birthday boy waking up with a sore head, walking around with a cup of coffee in one hand and a bag of crushed ice attached to his forehead. He. Needed. Kebabs. I couldn't believe my selfishness. I ran upstairs in my nicest pyjamas, handed over the leftovers with a feeble excuse and left him to fire up the Outback. He had sun and Seekh Kebabs. Summer was looking up at last.

Seekh Kebabs
Skewers of creamy ground lamb

I have a strict rule about eating Indian food at restaurants – always order what you can't easily rustle up at home. For years, Seekh Kebabs featured religiously as a restaurant favourite. The part about grinding meat and ending up with a soggy mess left me a little wobbly at the knees and weak in spirit when I considered attempting them at home.

As so often happens, the attempt was the biggest anticlimax ever. The mixture was soft but workable. The meat grinding a semi breeze. Manicured fingers easy enough to restore with a nailbrush and washing-up liquid. Best of all, there was no need to add oil! The hardest part was trying not to eat the soft batons of creamy ground meat entirely by myself.

Makes 15
8cm (3in) root ginger
12 garlic cloves
25g (1oz) fresh mint
25g (1oz) fresh coriander
1kg (2lb 3oz) minced lamb
1 large egg
3 tsp garam masala
1½ tsp chilli powder
½ tsp freshly ground nutmeg
2 tsp salt

15 bamboo skewers

1. Peel the ginger and garlic, pick the mint leaves from their stems and cut off the hard ends of the coriander stalks. Beat the egg in a small bowl.

2. In a food processor, whiz together the ginger, garlic and fresh herbs, along with one quarter of the mince and half the egg. You want to grind the meat to a smooth creamy paste. Remove this into a large mixing bowl and blitz another quarter of the meat with the remaining egg.

3. Now, add the remaining meat to the bowl, along with the spices and salt, and go in with your fingers, mixing the whole lot. You want the ground meat and the mince to integrate well together so no one notices that you cheated by not grinding half the mince.

4. Cover the bowl with a plate or cling film and chill in the fridge for at least an hour, or longer if possible. I had a quick beauty sleep.

5. When you're ready to go, dampen your hands and divide the mixture into 15 even-sized lumps. Moistening your hands under the tap will prevent the mixture from sticking to them. Likewise, soaking the bamboo skewers »

126

in water for 20 minutes will prevent them burning in the heat of the barbecue or grill. Then take each lump and shape it into a narrow sausage around one of the skewers. Keep wetting your palm to make this process as easy as possible.

6. Finally barbecue or grill each kebab at a high temperature for 20 minutes, turning every 5 minutes to ensure even cooking. Enjoy piping hot with green chutney. Preferably in the company of friends.

TOP RIGHT Hariyali Tikkis (page 135)
ABOVE RIGHT Seekh Kebabs (page 126)

ABOVE Cucumber and Mint Raita (page 115)

ABOVE Bharwan Shimla Mirch (page 138)

Tandoori Macchli
Moist barbecued monkfish in tandoori spices

I can't resist a good tandoori kebab. Instantly recognisable with their bright red colour and spicy aroma, these kebabs of marinated chicken, paneer or fish are best enjoyed in fresh air on a hot day.

For years, I simply used a packet of ready-made tandoori masala. When I plucked enough courage to make the masala myself, I discovered it was idiot-proof and far tastier than anything I'd ever used from a carton. The food colouring may not be to everyone's taste, but it feels a shame to leave it out when it's such a defining part of the kebab's character.

Feeds 4
600g (1lb 5oz) monkfish tails
5cm (2in) root ginger
6 garlic cloves
1 tsp coriander seeds
1 tsp cumin seeds
100g (3½oz) low-fat natural
    yoghurt
2 tsp chilli powder
1 tsp kasoori methi
    (dried fenugreek leaves)
½ tsp red food colouring
2 tbsp oil
juice of ½ lime
salt

4 bamboo skewers

1. Cut the monkfish into large bite-sized cubes and place in a bowl.

2. Peel the ginger and garlic, place in a food processor and whiz into a smooth paste with the coriander and cumin seeds and half the yoghurt. Add the rest of the yoghurt, the chilli powder, kasoori methi, food colouring and salt to the bowl of the food processor and whiz to a purée. If you don't have a food processor, you could just mix the masala powders with the chopped ginger and garlic in a bowl.

3. Check it for salt. You want this marinade to be overpowering in every way – salty, spicy, bitter – because cooking the fish will soften the taste.

4. Now, smother the monkfish with this marinade, making sure every piece is well coated. Then place in the fridge and leave to chill until you're ready for the barbecue. Two hours will be plenty. >>

5. When you're ready, thread on to skewers (soaking the skewers in water for 20 minutes will prevent them burning) and line up on the barbecue or under a hot grill. Mix the oil and lime juice together and baste the fish twice during cooking to prevent it from drying out. The kebabs will take about 10 minutes, but make sure you open one up and check that it is cooked through before feeding people!

6. Tandoori Macchli is perfect just on its own. But feel free to serve it with a mixed salad tossed in a lemony dressing and some hot naans.

Paneer Shashlik

Skewers of soft tandoori paneer, peppers and onion

I knew this recipe was going to be a firm family favourite when my brother-in-law's pet dog Harry started circling the barbecue with moist, hopeful eyes. We were running late from the day's activities. We had 20 minutes to get the food on plates and a fight with Harry on our hands before we did that.

Shashliks are skewered kebabs eaten across central Asia, Pakistan and northern India. I love the paneer version because of the killer combination of soft cheese with crunchy peppers and onions. You could fold them into ready-made naans and dip into green chutney, but I would highly recommend hot buttered basmati rice for a decadent twist.

Makes 8
Vegetarian
5cm (2in) root ginger
4 garlic cloves
1 tsp cumin seeds
1 tsp coriander seeds
100g (3½oz) low-fat natural
    yoghurt
2 tsp chilli powder
1 tsp kasoori methi
    (dried fenugreek leaves)
½ tsp red food colouring
225g (1oz) paneer
1 green pepper
1 red pepper
1 small red onion
juice of ½ lime
2 tbsp vegetable oil
salt

8 bamboo or metal skewers

1. First make the tandoori marinade. Peel the ginger and garlic and, using a food processor, whiz them into a smooth paste with the cumin and coriander seeds and the yoghurt. Mix in the chilli powder, kasoori methi, food colouring and salt to taste.

2. Now cut the paneer into 16 even, bite-sized pieces and leave to soak in the marinade. Meanwhile, halve and deseed the peppers and peel the onion, then cut up into chunks each about 2.5cm (1in) square and soak in a mixture of lime juice, salt and vegetable oil. Taste this marinade to make sure it delivers a strong kick, adding more salt if needed.

3. Next wet the bamboo skewers (if using) in cold water for 20 minutes so they don't burn and collapse on the barbecue. Thread the ingredients on to the skewers – pepper, onion, cube of paneer, pepper, onion and another cube of cheese. Repeat this with all eight skewers.

4. When the barbecue is ready, cook the skewers for about 10 minutes, turning regularly, until the peppers and onions get charred on the outside »

and the paneer softens to a mozzarella-like texture. Alternatively, place
the skewers under a hot grill and cook for the same length of time, again
turning regularly. Eat the kebabs straight away before the paneer goes cold.

WE'RE NOT ALWAYS SKULKING AROUND IN LONDON,
waiting for the sun to shine. Sometimes we have inspired ideas.
Like travelling to a small picturesque Cambridge village to destroy
the perfectly calm rural existence of the man's twin brother.

The thought of a weekend away from London had me running
for countryside essentials:

» **ANTIHISTAMINES** – Fresh air, foliage and house pets are a triple
allergy whammy.
» **FLAT SHOES** – For walking (good heavens!).
» **OVERSIZED SUNGLASSES** – Well, if we were finally going to have decent
weather …
» **A HANDFUL OF SPICES** – We'll be in a BIG house with its OWN garden.
What an opportunity!

The bags were packed. I threw myself with our other siblings into our
Knight Rider and we set off for Cambridge. The first few hours would be
spent punting down the River Cam. We were planning to make a mighty
splash amidst the many families, tourists and students who had all had the
same brilliant idea. The man's over-the-top, bafflingly Cambridge-educated
littlest brother was tasked with navigating us down the waterway.

It started well. I found a dry patch on which to perch my brand new
white shorts. Away from the smelly wet pole and the raucous screeches
that escaped the crazy punter. We managed to steer away from the base
without maiming anyone. But things quickly unravelled. Within minutes,
we had lost the pole. Once retrieved, with the help of a semi-naked student,
we proceeded to crash into most other punts heading back to the base.
And create enough noise to warrant an Asbo. I nodded back sympathetically
to the people in the other boats: *I don't know why they let him loose, either.*

By this time, the Cambridge-educated one was getting thirsty. Not content with upsetting the peace of most large groups around us, he identified a quiet couple to bother. They clearly knew what they were doing. But more importantly, they had a case brimming over with ice-cold Bacardi Breezers. Before we could say 'settle down', the irrepressible one had exchanged pleasantries, acquired a few bottles from them and jumped on to a low-lying branch in a Tarzan-like effort to board their boat. It was all too much. I sat quietly bemused. Praying I didn't bump into anyone I knew. Hoping that the dreaded journey would end. Wishing we could escape to the Japanese restaurant we'd booked for lunch.

But the evening was what I was really looking forward to – open-air theatre and picnic bags stuffed with nibbly foods, strawberries, chocolates and champagne. Rugs were spread out and hampers opened as we poured the champagne into disposable flutes. Tucked into the enormous spread and my Hariyali Tikkis – pea, spinach and potato croquettes. Luckily, the little brother was relatively calm after the morning's antics. And then the play began. The actors ranted and raved on stage, delivering dialogue like off-target arrows. A bizarre, masked fairy dance broke up the delirium. A surreal pantomime and tango performance weaved its way into the improvised script. Sending the audience into peals of laughter.

This was *A Midsummer Night's Dream*?

The siblings sat quietly, sniggering into their woollen scarves. Funnily enough, I'd lost my sense of humour. I was in the middle of nowhere. Dressed ridiculously in my Dorothy-esque red kitten heels and borrowed fleece. Watching a bunch of monkeys butchering Shakespeare. While cows provided backing vocals in the fields beyond. The final straw was when the actors requested picnic leftovers at the end of the performance. The cheek! While the Bard was turning in his grave? I grabbed the six leftover Hariyali Tikkis and ran to the car before anyone could say, 'Wherefore art thou?'

Indian picnic specialities are made up of spicy, tangy finger foods that you can snack on all day long. I remember Frankies – rotis stuffed with spicy potato mash – and cucumber and green chutney sandwiches enjoyed at roadside family picnics during the holidays. And the little vegetable tikkis and street-food bites that we carried to annual school outings. Making little snacks for 17 people, at a picnic or a party, calls for some dedication and forward planning. Which is why I make large quantities of a few recipes that can be oven-baked rather than shallow-fried in batches.

Hariyali Tikkis
Baked spinach, pea and ginger croquettes

It took me three days to decide on this healthy, easy and filling snack for the theatre picnic. Just as I unwrapped the foil tray they sat in, someone remarked, 'They're not much to look at, are they?'

'Never judge a book by its cover!' I snarled back. If appearances were everything, these little things wouldn't get a look-in. Speckled green, rough and ready, they're like the whacky-patterned shoes you acquired in the sales – the perfect accessory to liven up even the dullest ensemble.

Feeds 15–20

Vegetarian
1kg (2lb 3oz) frozen spinach
1kg (2lb 3oz) frozen peas
7 large potatoes
8cm (3in) root ginger
3 fresh green finger chillies
40g (1½oz) fresh
 coriander leaves
2 tbsp cornflour
2 tbsp oil
salt

1. In two separate pans, simmer the spinach and peas in boiling water for 5 minutes, or until the peas are soft and the spinach has defrosted and heated through. Peel, quarter and boil the potatoes for 15–20 minutes until they fall apart when prodded with a fork.

2. Drain the spinach, squeezing it well in your hands to get rid of all the water. Then put all the cooked vegetables in a large mixing bowl and leave to cool.

3. Next peel the ginger and chop finely, along with the chillies and coriander. Add all three ingredients to the vegetables in the mixing bowl. Add the cornflour and salt to taste, then mash the whole lot together with your hands. Check for salt, adding more if needed.

4. Stick this mixture in the fridge to cool and dry out until you're ready to cook the tikkis. I just helped get the drinks bagged up for the picnic in the meantime. When you're ready, preheat the grill to high and line a baking sheet with foil. Take 1 tablespoon of oil and spread it evenly over the base of the sheet.

5. Then divide the mixture into 15–20 even-sized balls, flatten each into a 4cm (1½in) disc and place on the baking sheet, leaving a 1cm (½in) gap between each. (Not all the tikkis will fit on to one sheet; you will need to cook them in two batches.) Place under the grill and cook for 12 minutes on one »

side, then turn over and cook for a further 12 minutes until the tikkis are pale brown on both sides.

6. You need to be careful when flipping them over, as they'll be soft and hot. If they fall apart, just shape them again on the sheet. You could just shallow-fry them for 8 minutes on either side, but this will take longer and use more oil.

7. Remove from the grill and place on a plate to cool, then repeat with another batch – first spreading more oil over the baking sheet – until all the mixture is used up. As the tikkis cool, they will harden and hold together better. These are a great hit stone cold dunked in Dhaniya Pudina chutney (see pages 120–1).

Lamb Chaaps
Succulent lamb chops drizzled with rose water

Butchers love me. Ruined by years of supermarket shopping, I never have a clue what I really want. Or need. As I flap around matching the best promotions with the wrong cuts of meat, they entertain themselves by palming me off with the most excessive pieces of lamb and goat.

Inevitably, I end up trying to justify the large hole in my wallet and the superior quality of ingredients with highly scented kebabs marinated in rich spices. Best saved for a small sunny gathering, these are the perfect outdoor treat and foil for my routine stupidity.

Feeds 8
4 large garlic cloves
5cm (2in) root ginger
4 green cardamoms
2.5cm (1in) cinnamon stick
1 dried long red chilli
½ tsp freshly ground nutmeg
2 tsp coriander powder
8 whole black peppercorns
1 heaped tbsp natural
    Greek yoghurt
8 lamb chops
2 tbsp rose water
salt

1. Peel the ginger and garlic and, using a food processor, purée with all the spices and the Greek yoghurt until smooth, adding enough salt to make a pungent marinade.

2. Smother the lamb chops with this marinade, place in a large bowl and leave to sit for 1–2 hours until you're ready to eat. Then barbecue the chops for 10 minutes on each side until cooked through. If the weather turns, or you don't have a barbecue, you could just cook them for the same amount of time under a hot grill.

3. Drizzle the rose water on to the sizzling chops before you serve them. They taste delicious with sliced onion rings steeped in lemon juice.

Bharwan Shimla Mirch
Baked peppers stuffed with masala lentils

I first made a batch of these for a friend when she came over for dinner armed with carrot cake and Oriental lilies. A high-flying corporate executive and keen cook, she found these were just the inspiration she needed to try her hand at Indian cooking.

Since then, I have made these for picnics, barbecues and even at teatime. Soft, sweet and juicy roasted peppers don't need to be talked up too much. But filled with crumbly, spiced lentils they make a fantastic and filling snack at any time.

Feeds 3–6
Vegetarian
200g (7oz) channa
  (split yellow) lentils
3 mixed peppers
1 pinch of asafoetida
1 tsp cumin seeds
1 tsp chilli powder
1 tsp coriander powder
½ tsp turmeric powder
3 tbsp oil
salt

1. Wash the channa lentils thoroughly in cold water and soak for 2–3 hours in twice as much water as lentils. I do this when I wake up in the morning, leaving the lentils until I'm ready to cook.

2. Run a sharp knife around the top of each pepper and yank out the middle. This will get rid of most of the seeds. Then halve each pepper.

3. After 2–3 hours, the lentils will have absorbed most of the water they were left to soak in. Coarsely grind them in a food processor with 2 tablespoons of the water they were soaked in, to get a thick paste. If you do this in two batches, it'll be infinitely quicker.

4. Preheat the oven to 200°C (400°F), gas mark 6.

5. Pour 2 tablespoons of the oil into a large frying pan set over a high heat. When the oil is hot, add (in the following order) the asafoetida, cumin seeds and spice powders. Sizzle for a few seconds, then mix in the ground lentils and stir viciously with a wooden spoon to combine them with the masala.

6. Keep cooking for about 15 minutes until the lentils darken to a rich ochre and their aroma changes. They will keep getting stuck to the »

bottom of the pan as they cook, but just scrape them off with the wooden spoon. Once the lentils are cooked, add salt to taste.

7. Next, line a baking sheet with foil and evenly spread with the remaining tablespoon of oil. Stuff each half of pepper with the lentil filling, then quarter with a sharp knife, place on a baking sheet and roast for 30 minutes until the top of each piece of stuffed pepper is crusty and golden.

8. Wrap the peppers up in the foil they were cooked in and serve with a mint and yoghurt dip. (Make as for the Cucumber and Mint Raita on page 115, omitting the cucumber.)

5.

SHOWING OFF

Recipes for special occasions
and for impressing guests

Miss Masala.

ARRIVING HOME after one seemingly never-ending Monday at work,
I frantically started ripping off my suit and wrapping five metres of chiffon
around myself. We had been invited to an Indian wedding out in suburbia.
Where I would face a thousand uncles and aunties, all of whom
wholeheartedly disapproved of the *bona fide* white man I call a husband.

It made the day's one irate supplier, two tense client meetings and three
deadlines seem positively inconsequential in comparison.

I slipped on large diamond earrings and very, very high gold stilettos.
Ammunition. I was ready. The man and I drove out into the depths of
commuter countryside. The London A-Z was no good here. Passports would
be more appropriate. We were beyond Zone 2. More worryingly – we were
lost. Following instructions from an amused local resident, we finally wove
down a narrow country lane towards our destination.

It was breathtaking. The driveway opened into acres of rolling countryside,
with a beautiful Jain temple to one side. Jainism is one of the oldest religions
in India, characterised by a philosophy of renunciation of worldly
possessions and undesirable traits like anger, pride and greed, by reverence
for all living creatures, and by spiritual enlightenment. Dragging our eyes
from the stunning architecture, we approached the community centre that
would host the reception. A large sign greeted us: 'No smoking, drinking
alcohol or eating non-vegetarian food'.

Gulp. Our lives were temporarily over.

I nervously shuffled into the packed centre, holding on to the man for dear life. If we got separated, how would he find me? Did they have a lost and found counter? And then I got 'the look'. Not one, but many. Was it directed at the gora chokro draped on my right arm or at the exquisite, hand-embroidered black saree draped over my left?

No time to think. We quickly located my Cambridge-educated brother-in-law and his friends. Jostled through the crowds to wave hello to the bride and groom. By which time, we were starving. The queue for food stretched all the way from the buffet table in the basement to the top of stairs.

No surprise there. Indian weddings are famed for ostentation, high glamour and excessive consumption of food. Whether there is also drink depends on which community the betrothed belong to. The next wedding I attended, which took place in London at the Institute of Directors, was a case in point.

Home to UK plc, the IoD is usually a sea of suits bobbing around the building and quietly hosting meetings in nooks and corners. I felt strangely out of place entering it in a rich bronze and peacock blue salwar kameez. And I wasn't the only one feeling like that. The staff didn't know what had hit them. Faced as they were with 500 suited and bejewelled Indians, all their little terrors and a four-piece, turbaned live band. It was a party like no other they had seen.

As the little ones pelted guests with paper cups, napkins and bits of food from the top of the palatial staircase, I decided enough was enough. I needed a drink. Mercifully, this wedding had a selection of alcoholic goodies on offer. Grabbing husband by the arm, I squeezed through the glittering guests to the bar.

Three gorgeous girls ahead of me in exquisite, sequinned, floor-length skirts known as lehengas requested apple juice, orange juice and, gasp, sparkling wine. The pressure was immense.

'I'll have vodka lemonade, please.'

'Single or double?'

'Double, please. Not too much lemonade.' I needed a stiff drink to survive this.

'For *you* madam?'

Was that a hint of disapproval in his voice?

Suddenly, to a microphone announcement and a flurry of activity, the floor-to-ceiling curtains at the end of the room parted, presenting the new husband and wife. They cut a cake. Thanked guests. And then made the most welcome speech: 'Dinner is served.' The room emptied within minutes as hoards of wedding guests clambered to the food.

Attending Indian weddings takes me right back to my own. We were so young. If we had known what being married actually meant, we may not have bothered. The bride's side of the family travelled from Kolkata, the groom's from Peru, Croydon and Oxbridge. Mother pointed out that white is the colour of mourning in India. So I wore acid pink, in church.

We exchanged vows in a little country church in Stubbings in Berkshire and then drove down to the best-ever summer garden party – our reception. Forty people, crates of Pommery champagne and 90s dance music. Shame Granddad spoke entirely about himself when he made the father of the bride's speech.

Six months later, we travelled to India to hold a 'small' wedding reception – only 350 of my mother's closest friends and family. Of course, I wasn't having any of that red saree, gold jewellery and vermillion powder on my forehead to proclaim my new marital status malarkey. Or the tear-jerking sitar music that echoes the sorrow the bride is meant to feel for leaving home as a married woman. I was deliriously happy to leave home. Only something upbeat, uplifting and progressive would suit the mood.

Three hours later, I understood the real meaning of the tearful music. It is played to reflect the throbbing pain in the bride's jaw as she smiles for the hundredth time at a complete stranger, accepting a gift that she will never use.

I wanted a strong drink. I received another Persian rug.

It's the rich, aromatic and lovingly prepared special-occasion biryanis, curries and dals that keep me going at Indian weddings, my own included. When, for religious reasons, alcohol isn't served, sugar is the next best thing. This must be why dessert is such an important part of any Indian wedding meal. Surely, a buffet table filled with sweets is the traditionally acceptable equivalent of a line of tequila shots? (For a whole chapter of sweet treats, turn to pages 214–39.) A touch of sweetness added to a savoury old familiar such as dal or naan can also transform them into something fit for a wedding or other special event.

Sweet or savoury, give me a bellyful of wedding feast and I'm ready to show off my Bollywood moves.

Cholar Dal
Sweet and spicy coconut and raisin lentils

Bengali weddings are incomplete without two things: routine jokes about bodily functions, and this rich and complex dal. You sit on rickety chairs by wooden tables, while waiters serve measured spoonfuls of Cholar Dal on banana-leaf plates. Just as you're about to scoop the dal up with luchi – light, fluffy, flaky little Indian breads (known in the north as 'pooris') – the inappropriate jokes commence.

As with a lot of other Bengali dishes, this dal has a hint of sweetness and is best enjoyed thick and piping hot. The ghee is not optional. Leave it out and you'll miss an important ingredient of this celebratory wonder.

Feeds 4
Vegetarian
250g (9oz) channa
  (split yellow) lentils
½ tsp cumin powder
½ tsp coriander powder
1 tsp turmeric powder
½ tsp granulated sugar
2 tbsp ghee
2 tbsp diced fresh coconut
1 tsp garam masala
½ tsp chilli powder
1 fresh green finger chilli
2 tbsp raisins
salt

1. Wash the lentils thoroughly in a sieve under cold running water. Transfer them to a large pan, adding three times as much cold water as lentils.

2. Bring the lentils to the boil. When they start bubbling, add the cumin, coriander, turmeric and sugar and boil until the lentils are soft to the touch but still intact. This should take a good 30 minutes. But don't wander off – the lentils may bubble over. If they do, just take off the heat for a few seconds and stir ferociously.

3. Now push the lentils to the edge of the pan and mash them up with a wooden spoon. You will need to do this about four times to ensure the lentils are mashed enough to thicken the dal. In a separate little pan, heat the ghee on a high setting and when hot add the diced coconut, garam masala, chilli powder and green finger chilli. Fry for 30 seconds and then add to the lentils. Stir in the raisins and some salt to taste. Voila!

Paneer Butter Masala
Soft cheese in a rich and creamy curry

I've eaten hundreds of varieties of paneer, but this particular recipe is best enjoyed at a roadside dhaba, or food shack, found on the highways around Delhi or in Punjab. You sit on a bench in between several menacing truck drivers, and pay three times as much as any of them for the joy of tucking into the real buttery deal.

Traditionally, the key to perfecting this dish is a large quantity of fat – cream, butter and ground nuts. But there is a middle path that doesn't require the consumption of a week's fat allowance in one sitting. My trick is to use thick Greek yoghurt instead of cream and a limited amount of butter. If the occasion demands, however, by all means go mad and revert to cream instead.

Feeds 4

Vegetarian
250g (9oz) paneer
½ tsp chilli powder
½ tsp turmeric powder
1 tsp kasoori methi
  (dried fenugreek leaves)
2 garlic cloves
1cm (½in) root ginger
1 tbsp ghee
1 bay leaf
1 heaped tsp
  coriander powder
2 tbsp tomato purée
4 tbsp natural Greek yoghurt
10 cashew nuts
½ tsp garam masala
1 tbsp butter
salt

1. Dice the paneer into pieces each 1cm (½in) wide and 2cm (¾in) long. Mix ¼ teaspoon each of the chilli and turmeric powder into the diced paneer, along with ½ teaspoon of salt.

2. Meanwhile, soak the kasoori methi in a teaspoon of hot water, then peel the garlic and ginger and purée to a fine paste with 2 tablespoons of water using a hand blender. In a medium pan, heat the ghee on a high setting. When it is hot, add the masala-coated paneer and fry for 2 minutes on one side and 2 minutes on the opposite side, or until pale brown on both sides. This will seal in the spices and prevent the paneer from falling apart in the curry later.

3. Remove the paneer pieces with a slotted spoon and, in the same fat, fry the bay leaf. Within seconds, the bay leaf will start sizzling. When this happens, add the ginger and garlic purée and stir gently for 2 minutes until it turns translucent. »

4. Now add the coriander and the remaining chilli and turmeric, along with the tomato purée, and stir vigorously for about 2 minutes until the pungent smell of the masala softens. Then spoon in the yoghurt, lower the heat and simmer for 5 minutes. You will see the colour of the yoghurt change from creamy white to a rich red as the spices blend into it.

5. In the meantime, using a hand blender, grind the cashew nuts into a fine paste with a tablespoon of hot water. Stir it into the masala along with the paneer pieces, the garam masala and the kasoori methi, together with its water. These are added to balance the tangy taste of the curry. Give them a good 2 minutes on a low simmer to do their magic.

6. To finish, stir in the butter and salt to your taste and enjoy piping hot with some aromatic pulao (see the box on pages 170–1).

Patra ni Macchi
Marinated cod steamed in banana-leaf parcels

Patra ni Macchi is a Parsi wedding staple served on the day of the actual ceremony, following four days of pre-festivities. The Parsis have been the subject of much debate in recent years due to their dwindling numbers. To me they are the Indian community that gave us the genius of Freddie Mercury, the business success that is Tata Group, and one of the finest cuisines in India.

I got a version of this recipe from my Parsi neighbour's own cookbook – a venerable relic inherited from her mother. By the time she got it back, a few more pages were hanging off its delicate spine. But I'd had a chance to perfect this simple, flavourful, special-occasion classic using conveniently frozen banana leaves and coconut, both of which I sourced in Chinatown.

Feeds 6
6 cod fillets, skinned and all bones removed
6 large banana leaves
3 garlic cloves
6 fresh green finger chillies
6 tbsp fresh or frozen grated coconut
50g (2oz) fresh coriander leaves
25g (1oz) fresh mint leaves
3 tbsp freshly squeezed lemon juice
salt

1. Wash each cod fillet well under cold running water, dabbing dry on kitchen paper. Wash the banana leaves, taking care not to split the delicate fibres.

2. Peel the garlic and, using a blender or food processor, purée into a paste with the remaining ingredients, adding salt to taste. The marinade should be strong and punchy in every way.

3. Place each fish fillet on a banana leaf and smother with the marinade. Then wrap it as neatly as you can and set aside. You don't need to tie it with thread because the steaming process will seal the parcel shut.

4. When you're ready to eat, steam each banana-leaf parcel for 7–10 minutes, open side facing down, using a steamer, or a colander covered with a pan lid and placed over a large pan of boiling water. The fish should be moist but cooked through. (Open just one parcel first to check if cooked.)

5. This is a wonderful way to impress guests and can be eaten alongside Parsi Brown Rice (see the box on pages 170–1). Or serve with Khichdi (see page 194) for a super-healthy meal.

Chingri Malai Curry
King prawns in a sweet coconut curry

You've never seen large prawns until you've had Golda Chingri Malai Curry at a Bengali wedding. These giant specimens of the crustacean clan are cooked in their shells and served on the customary banana leaves with Ghee Bhaat or plain rice. Unless you're one of the lucky sons-in-law, in which case your exalted status will earn you a solid silver plate and a matching shiny cup.

The simplicity of this recipe typifies classic Bengali cooking. Buy the best-quality raw king prawns you can afford. I normally get an economy bag of frozen king prawns in the Oriental grocery stores in Chinatown. Take your time cooking the masala paste. And savour every mouthful!

Feeds 4
1 large onion
1cm (½in) root ginger
1 medium tomato
1 tbsp mustard oil
1 tbsp sunflower oil
whole spices
  1 bay leaf
  4 cloves
  2.5cm (1in) cinnamon stick
½ tsp granulated sugar
1 tsp chilli powder
1½ tsp turmeric powder
1 x 400ml can of reduced-fat
  coconut milk
400g (14oz) raw shelled
  king prawns
salt

1. Peel the onion and ginger, cut into chunks and purée in a blender or food processor. Chop the tomato into little pieces.

2. Pour both oils into a large frying pan set over a high heat and, when hot, add the whole spices and the sugar. When the sugar caramelises to a lovely reddish brown, add the onion and ginger paste and fry over a high heat, stirring regularly. In about 15 minutes, the paste will start losing its pungent smell and turn a pale shade of brown.

3. Next, add the chilli, turmeric and chopped tomato. Now comes the only tricky part of the recipe. You just have to fry all this until the onion mixture oozes oil and is smooth in texture and cooked when tasted. This will take another 20 minutes at least, so hang in there.

4. Now add the coconut milk, reduce the heat and simmer for about 10 minutes. Then add the prawns, stirring gently for about 5 minutes until they have cooked through. Add salt to taste and serve immediately. If your guests aren't due until the next day, you could make the curry sauce in advance and add the prawns just before serving.

WEDDINGS I CAN MANAGE. But religious functions call for a whole
new set of survival techniques.

In India, my Hindu family celebrated several religious festivals, or pujas,
with great aplomb. And there was no shortage of gods and goddesses to choose
from. We had Diwali, the festival of lights and sound, with offerings to Ganesh
and Lakshmi, the celestial representations of wealth and prosperity; Kali Puja, in
which the fearsome Mother Goddess was evoked; Saraswati Puja, which saw us
children feverishly offer textbooks and notebooks to be blessed by the Goddess
of knowledge; and there was Holi, a riotous celebration of the playful god Krishna,
with paint smearing and adults drinking bhang, a cannabis-laced milkshake.

And why stop there? Any excuse for a celebration! We honoured the
festivals of other religions with equal fervour. At Christmas, it was off to
New Market to buy plastic trees, stuffed Santas and decorative candies.
On Eid ul-Fitr, marking the end of Ramadan or the Islamic Holy Month
of Fasting, we got all dressed up and marched down to the home of our
chauffeur Idris dada for a feast fit for a Mughal emperor.

It took me 14 years to muster up enough courage to admit that I
wasn't sure God existed. My parents were not the least bit offended by
the revelation. As long as I was still prepared to join in the fun.

Little has changed since. Once a year, I seek out the thrills of the biggest
event of the Bengali religious calendar at Camden Town Hall. I'm talking
about Durga Puja, five days of worship devoted to the symbol of motherhood,
female power, and good over evil. This is when London's entire Bengali
community descends on this one massive venue to identify suitable
marriage partners, keep up with the Chatterjees, and, of course, pray.

Sis and I braved lashing rain and the London Underground in full Indian
festive gear. The annual reconnect-with-our-Bengali-brethren event had
officially commenced. Outside King's Cross tube station, we followed a trail
of aunties in sarees and uncles in woollen balaclavas to the puja. Inside, it was
like we had been transported back to India. Crowds of women stood praying in
front of the stage with folded hands and bent heads. Men stood around talking
politics, weather and planned trips to the Motherland. Meanwhile, their sprogs
ran around terrorising innocent bystanders. And young people eyed each
other up.

Dressed in matching deep red salwar kameezes, high heels and overcoats,
Sis and I were attracting some attention. She tossed her hair from side to

side with the ease of a Bollywood starlet and career upstart. Still single at 22, this was her moment to snare a 'bhodro bhalo chele', or well-behaved, good boy. The ultimate trophy husband for a girl from a 'decent' family. Sadly, she was about as interested in finding a lifelong partner at this event as getting a midwinter Brazilian bikini wax.

I, on the other hand, froze solid. A toothy grin caught my eye. What a waste! I was neither bhodro nor bhalo. And already long married. I strategically raised my left hand to flash the ring. A quarter carat, the diamond had been purchased on a student loan. It had its work cut out for the evening. Would standing under the bright lights draw sufficient attention to it? By this time, I had spotted some old Bengali acquaintances and the pleasantries began.

'Hello, how are you?'

'How is your other half/love interest?'

'How have you been recently?' Cue details about recent illnesses, exotic holidays, career moves.

'Aren't your children beautiful/intelligent/energetic?' (Delete as appropriate.)

By this time, a queue was forming for the highlight of our evening – the bhog, or food offering. Durga Puja bhog is a simple feast of rice and lentil khichuri, deep-fried vegetables and mishti. As with much of temple cooking in India, the food is prepared with the principles of sattvic yoga in mind, in order to promote good thoughts and positive energy (i.e. nothing sexual). No onions and garlic, therefore.

Most intriguing. But for Sis and me there's something about standing in the mile-long queue and sizing up the crowds that makes eating a miniscule portion of food from a foil carton ten times more special than how it tastes. We were just making for the queue when someone broke my reverie with 'Don't leave now', rattling off the names of a dozen other long-lost Bengalis just about to arrive. Sis and I exchanged a quick look. Made our excuses. And jumped into the food queue for the blessed meal.

Divine intervention – just the way it should be.

Bhoger Khichuri
Traditional Durga Puja rice and lentils

Sis and I can't have enough of puja bhog. Ever since she arrived in England, we've been faithfully making annual trips to London's Camden Town Hall for a foil tray of the rice and lentil dish cooked especially for the occasion. She, the student, doesn't get much decent food. But I have no excuse really.

Once when we had battled through biting winds and pouring rain on a busy weekday to get to the divine offering, things were suspiciously quiet. The main doors to the venue were bolted shut. Turned out that puja had concluded the day before! We legged it to the nearest Indian vegetarian buffet, and I recreated the bhog for us the following weekend.

Feeds 4
Vegetarian
100g (3½oz) masoor (split red) lentils
1 large potato
1 small cauliflower
100g (3½oz) basmati rice
1 tsp turmeric powder
1 tsp grated root ginger
1 handful of frozen peas
2 tbsp ghee
4 fresh green finger chillies
3 bay leaves
2.5cm (1in) cinnamon stick
4 green cardamoms
1 tsp granulated sugar
1 tsp garam masala
salt

1. Place the lentils in a sieve and rinse thoroughly under a cold tap. While they are draining, peel the potato and cut into small bite-sized cubes, then cut the cauliflower into similar-sized florets.

2. In a large pan, dry-roast the lentils over a high heat for 1 minute until they give off a wonderful warm aroma. Then add the same quantity of hot water as lentils and bring to the boil. In the meantime, rinse the rice well. When the lentils start bubbling, mix in the rice, turmeric and grated ginger, and add a mug of hot water.

3. Cook for 2 minutes, then stir in the potato, followed after 4–5 minutes by the cauliflower and peas. Let the whole mixture keep bubbling on a medium heat until the lentils are squishy and integrate with the rice to form a thick soup. This will take about 20 minutes. Keep adding warm water so you get a runny consistency.

4. Take the pan off the hob. Make the tadka by heating the ghee in a small pan on a high setting. Slit the chillies lengthways. When the ghee starts sizzling, add these plus all the remaining ingredients except the garam masala. As the sugar caramelises, stir the tadka into the dal along with the garam masala. Add salt to taste and serve hot with Beguni (see page 156).

AYURVEDIC COOKING

JUST AS I BEGAN MASTERING THE ART OF COOKING INDIAN FOOD
AT HOME, MY MOTHER DECIDED TO FOX ME WITH A BOOK ON AYURVEDIC
COOKING. THIS TEAR-JERKINGLY ILL-WRITTEN TEXT WAS ENOUGH TO PUT
ME OFF AYURVEDIC COOKING FOR LIFE, NEVER MIND THE SCIENCE BEHIND
IT. AS IF IT WASN'T HARD ENOUGH TO EAT ONE COOKED MEAL A DAY
WITHOUT HAVING TO WORRY ABOUT THE UNIVERSAL INTELLIGENCE
OF THE PHYSIOLOGICAL PROCESS OF EATING. AND NO, I DON'T
KNOW WHAT THAT MEANS EITHER.

AYURVEDA IS AN ANCIENT INDIAN MEDICAL SYSTEM DATING
BACK TO 3000 BC. FROM WHAT I UNDERSTAND:

Every one of us has a body type, or 'dosha',
which governs our physical and mental well being.

The three doshas of Vata, Pitta or Kapha are formed from
the five elements that make up our universe. They tend
to be present in all of us in some combination,
with one more dominant than the others.

Vata governs the three primary doshas and is made up of
air and space. Fire and water govern Pitta, while water and
earth make up Kapha. The attributes of each dosha, along with
the specific combination of each within us determines our
physical, mental and emotional state.

You can take an online test to see what your dosha is.

Ill-health is a direct result of these forces
being out of balance.

Taste is an important way to stimulate the
nervous system and balance the doshas.

Ayurveda recognises six tastes: sweet, sour,
salty, pungent, bitter and astringent.

Pungent, salty and sour tastes produce a heating
effect on the body, while sweet, bitter and astringent
tastes have a cooling effect.

How we eat is also most important: lunch should be
the main meal of the day; we should eat slowly
and calmly in order to aid digestion.

While meat is not strictly forbidden,
Ayurvedic cooking promotes vegetarianism.

THIS IS WHERE I ZONE OUT. I CAN'T LIVE WITHOUT MEAT.
AND I CAN LIVE WITHOUT FURTHER DIETARY COMPLICATIONS.

Beguni
Crispy aubergine fritters

Khichuri is incomplete without awful weather and a serving of something bhaja, or 'fried'. In Kolkata monsoons, we would sit in the comfort of our living rooms playing cards, listening to old Bollywood tunes and eating khichuri, beguni, aloo bhaja and papads. While blocked drains and knee-high water brought the city to a standstill outside.

The trick to frying aubergines quickly and with minimum oil is to soak them in cold salted water beforehand. My dad taught me that this prevents them from absorbing all the oil in the pan and lying around uselessly for ages, refusing to cook. The aubergine slices here are cooked in a delicately spiced batter so you won't notice any discoloration of the flesh. Just fry as you're about to eat them so they're hot and crispy.

Feeds 4
Vegetarian
1 small aubergine
100g (3½oz) besan or gram (chickpea) flour
1 tsp nigella seeds
1 tsp salt
½ tsp chilli powder
5 tbsp oil

1. Cut the aubergine in half lengthways and then into slices 0.5cm (¼in) thick. Soak them in cold water while the khichuri (see page 153) is cooking.

2. When the khichuri is done, sift the besan flour through a fine sieve into a medium mixing bowl to remove any lumps. Then add all the other ingredients and stir in sufficient water, 1 tablespoon at a time, to create a thick batter with the consistency of a low-fat fruit yoghurt.

3. Pour the oil into a large frying pan set over a high heat. When the oil starts sizzling, dip each aubergine slice into the batter and shallow-fry, for 2 minutes on each side, until crisp and golden brown. Set them to rest on a thick napkin or kitchen paper to drain off any excess oil before you devour them with the khichuri.

Quick Lamb Biryani
Special aromatic spiced lamb and rice for Eid

Biryani is one of the original Mughal delicacies – an aromatic feast of rice and meat that is slow-cooked for hours and traditionally served at Eid. My earliest memories of it are when my dad cooked it at home. We sisters waited patiently for lunch until 4 pm, by which time we were ready to rip the flour-sealed lid off the darn thing and eat it directly out of the enormous cauldron it was baking in.

How I miss those days! Now I have to wait until trips to India, when my mother gets a special biryani chef in to make enough for lunch, dinner and breakfast for three days. My recipe is a cheat's version, noticeably quicker and with a vastly reduced ingredients list. But it'll impress nonetheless.

Feeds 4–6
2 tbsp milk
1 tsp saffron
5 medium onions
12 tbsp ghee
2 tbsp rose water
salt

For the dry masala
1 mace flower
4 cloves
4 green cardamoms
¼ tsp freshly ground nutmeg

For the lamb
1kg (2lb 3oz) diced
  shoulder of lamb
10 garlic cloves
5cm (2in) root ginger
3 fresh green finger chillies
15g (½oz) fresh coriander
  leaves
2 tsp cumin seeds
1 mace flower
1 tsp freshly ground nutmeg
1 tsp chilli powder
1 tsp garam masala
500g (1lb 2oz) natural
  Greek yoghurt
salt

For the rice
4 cloves
2 brown cardamoms
2.5cm (1in) cinnamon stick
500g (1lb 2oz) basmati rice

1. Warm the milk and soak the saffron in it. Next make the dry masala by crushing the mace flower, cloves and green cardamoms in a coffee grinder, mix with the nutmeg and set aside.

2. Now make the marinade for the lamb. Place the diced meat in a medium mixing bowl. Peel the ginger and garlic and, using a blender or food processor, purée with the remaining ingredients to make a thick marinade, adding salt to taste. Add this to the lamb, stirring so that the pieces of meat are well coated, and leave to sit while you prepare the rest of the dish.

3. Peel and finely slice the onions. In a medium pan, heat 8 tablespoons of the ghee on a high setting. When it is hot, add three of the chopped onions and sauté for 15 minutes until golden.

4. Next add the lamb and all of its masala, browning the meat all over. Lower the heat to medium, cover with a lid and cook, stirring frequently, until the meat is tender. This will take about 45 minutes, depending »

on the quality of the lamb. If the meat dries out during cooking, add half
a mug of hot water to moisten it and help it cook. Add salt to taste when
it's ready.

5. In the meantime, prepare the rice. In a large pan, heat 1 tablespoon of
the ghee on a high setting. When it's hot, sizzle the whole spices for a few
seconds and add the rice. Stir for 1 minute until it starts turning translucent,
and then add three mugs of water, cover with a lid and simmer for 5 minutes
until half cooked. Drain the water and leave to sit.

6. In a small frying pan, heat the remaining ghee on a high setting.
When it is hot, fry the remaining onions for 15 minutes until golden brown.

7. Now assemble and finish the biryani. Spread half the partly cooked rice
over the bottom of a casserole dish. Sprinkle half the dry masala over this,
along with half the fried onions, rose water and saffron milk. Spread the
lamb curry on top. Finally, layer with the remaining rice, dry masala, rose
water and saffron milk. Seal this tightly with the lid – if it's a bit wobbly,
wrap foil tightly around the edges.

8. Place on a low heat for 20 minutes until the rice is thoroughly cooked
and fluffy. Alternatively, place in the oven, preheated to 180°C (350°F),
gas mark 4, and cook for a similar length of time. Then scatter with the
remaining fried onions and serve piping hot, using a small plate to scoop
up the biryani from the bottom of the pot to ensure that everyone gets a bit
of everything. Serve with Anda Raita (see opposite).

Anda Raita

Egg raita tempered with curry leaves and whole spices (trust me!)

This recipe actually has nothing to do with Eid, when Bhurani Raita, yoghurt spiced with mint and chilli, is more traditionally served with biryani, alongside a fresh onion and tomato salad. My crazy friend Boobie discovered Anda Raita at a dinner party in India. Since then, it has become her signature dish. And one that I ritually use to shake guests out of their comfort zone.

Anda Raita completes any meal – from quiet TV suppers to elaborate feasts. It's wholesome enough to be a stand-alone side dish, served on its own as a light meal or snack with pitta bread, and will never fail to raise an eyebrow or two when given to guests. Besides, the ingredients are always readily available. One quick trip to the corner shop, curry leaves from the freezer and I'm always ready to spread Boobie's madness.

Feeds 6–8

Vegetarian
6 medium eggs
750g (1lb 10oz) low-fat
   natural yoghurt
3 tbsp oil
½ tsp asafoetida
1 heaped tsp cumin seeds
1½ tsp mustard seeds
½ tsp turmeric powder
4 dried long red chillies
15 curry leaves, fresh
   or frozen
salt

1. Place the eggs in a large pan of cold water set over a high heat and cook for 8 minutes until hard-boiled. Mix salt to taste in the yoghurt and pour into a shallow serving dish.

2. When the eggs are done, rinse them with cold running water, leave to sit for 2 minutes, then peel and halve them. Dunk the egg halves in the dish, ensuring they are smothered with the yoghurt.

3. Next make the tadka. Pour the oil into a little pan – set over a high heat. When it's hot, add the asafoetida and then quickly add the cumin and mustard seeds, turmeric and chillies. Wait for a few seconds, then add the curry leaves and watch them sizzle up.

4. Cook for 30 seconds, take the pan off the heat and pour the tadka evenly over the eggs and yoghurt. Enjoy this with biryani or Chicken Pulao (see page 75).

ABOVE CENTRE Lamb Biryani (page 157)
ABOVE RIGHT Patra Ni Macchi (page 148)

ABOVE LEFT Vodka Chilli Cocktails (page 177)

ABOVE Anda Raita (page 159)

TOP Cholar Dal (page 145)

ABOVE Jardaloo Sali Boti (page 165)

I LOVE A RAUCOUS DINNER PARTY. And the standards are
pretty high if my parents' ones are anything to go by.

Dad made his first meal aged ten. He's a passionate cook. And the official anti-Christ of anything remotely quick. Since his divorce from Mother, he has created a shrine to the art of authentic Indian home cooking in the form of a palatial kitchen. Endless granite and marble. Two cookers. A floor-standing clay tandoor. Even his main chef has two assistants. All three of them run ragged around him, chopping, stirring and tidying. While Dad navigates boxes of exotic spices sourced from far-flung corners of India. When he emerges from the kitchen six hours later with an eight-part meal, I can't help feeling a bit exhausted just at the sight of it.

I, on the other hand, have a tried and trusted approach to my soirées:

» Buy plenty of alcohol.
» Make one chicken/lamb curry and a dal.
» Serve it with a substantial yoghurt raita, which also cleverly doubles up as the vegetable dish, and a basmati rice pulao.
» Get sweets from an Indian shop or make Bhapa Doi (see page 231).
» Keep vanilla ice cream handy to douse any fiery bellies.

A gazillion dinners later, I should be the queen of the perfect party. The effortless hostess with an eye for detail and a dab hand at getting food on the table. No such luck, sadly. Guest dinners in the London Basu residence continue to be a regular but frantic occurrence.

Like the one I planned on Friday the 13th. Call me superstitious, but I had one bust-up at work, followed by a tough client meeting and then I slipped over in my patent winklepickers and grazed my knee. With each successive incident, I looked forward to the evening of ten friends just that little bit less.

I was afraid. Very afraid. And couldn't concentrate all day. I kept thinking: Will I accidentally leave the long-stemmed lilies at work? Will I be exposed as a lying fake with a bleeding knee as I burn the pre-prepared food while trying to reheat it in the oven? Will I get drunk before dinner is served, again? This time as a result of an antihistamine overdose and not excessive alcohol consumption … but I had to be strong. The food was cooked. It was too late to cancel now.

I rushed home with the lilies at 6 pm sharp. The food was ready to go.
I just needed to grill aubergines for the raita. Stick the Pyrex dishes of curry
into the oven. Ditch the work garb in favour of denim and Havaianas.
Then welcome my guests, smile on face, champagne in hand.

Of course, it is never that simple. The precooked lamb curry was still
partly frozen. Nowhere near ready to be reheated. I drained and shoved the
sliced aubergines under the grill. Started racing around the flat, placing
flowers in vases and picking magazines off the floor. Then the first guests
arrived. On time.

Forgetting the food for a moment, I welcomed them at the door. Showed
them the new design features in our flat. And then led them into the *pièce
de résistance* – the monochrome kitchen, complete with a dwarf-sized dining
table and temperamental but trendy black glass extractor. By this time, dark
clouds of black smoke had filled the space. The aubergines were on fire. My
friends, now seated, tried not to look alarmed. I plunged into action; flapping
the tea towel around in a lame attempt to improve air circulation
and prevent the smoke alarm from deafening the entire
neighbourhood. Meanwhile, timed to perfection, the door buzzer
went off, announcing the arrival of the remaining guests.

A smoky kitchen and frazzled aubergines were nothing a few
bottles of wine couldn't fix. Fresh air and cigarette smoke slowly
replaced the burnt smell, thanks to the smokers huddled on the
balcony. Hubby's Irish, Indian-food-hating best mate arrived
unannounced, having locked himself out of his own place.
Within an hour, the group had collectively knocked over a
bottle of red wine, smashed two glasses and permanently
disfigured my Conran fruit bowl.

When dinner was finally served, we settled down;
squashed around a table designed for four. Talking cars,
epilators, love and life, and devouring baingan raita,
Jardaloo Saali Boti and Jeera Pulao at breakneck speed.
Once everyone was fed, things improved. I was reinstated
as the ordinary mortal's undisputed queen of Indian home
cooking. My guests were drunk. I sat back and hit the bottle.

MY TOP FIVE DINNER PARTY POOPERS

BURK HUDSON ONCE SAID, 'PERFECTION IS A ROAD, NOT A
DESTINATION.' HOW TRUE. FOR ALL THE HUNDRED DINNER
PARTIES I HOST EVERY YEAR, I STILL ALWAYS FIND MYSELF
A LITTLE BIT UNPREPARED FOR MY GUESTS.

HERE'S WHERE I SLIP UP:

1.
Dinner taken out of the freezer too late and still
rock solid an hour before guests are due to arrive.

2.
Food put in the oven too late and still heating
well past respectable dinner time.

3.
Too many things left to do on the day — raita to be assembled,
pulao to be cooked, guests requiring entertainment.

4.
Garnishes overlooked — sprinkles of fresh coriander
and drizzles of lemon juice are too complicated in the
grand scheme of things.

5.
And that old chestnut: too much alcohol
consumed before the dinner is served.

NO DOUBT YOU WILL FARE MUCH BETTER.

Jardaloo Sali Boti
Tender lamb shank curry with apricots

Mother has developed more than a theoretical interest in cooking over recent years. Now she arrives in London every summer armed with contact lens solution, a caseful of spices and a wealth of interesting recipes. Which she then copies into my battered notebook with useful instructions (not) like: 'Add usual dhaniya, jeera masalas.'

Cryptic directions apart, her recipe for a rich, sweet and sour Parsi lamb shank curry has turned into one of my signature dishes for small parties. The ingredients are store-cupboard basics and shanks are one of the more common cuts of lamb available. Better still, the chips and rice they are served with form the basis of a complete meal. No need for any extras!

Feeds 4

whole spices
8 black peppercorns
5cm (2in) cinnamon stick
8 green cardamoms
4cm (1½in) root ginger
4 fat garlic cloves
2 medium onions
2 medium tomatoes
4 tbsp oil
½ tsp cumin powder
1 tsp coriander powder
½ tsp chilli powder
4 lamb shanks
 (about 750g/1lb 10oz
 in total)
2 large potatoes
1 tsp granulated sugar
3 drops of Worcestershire
 sauce
20 dried apricots
salt

1. Preheat the oven to 200°C (400°F), gas mark 6.

2. Place the whole spices on a baking sheet and dry-roast for 30 seconds until the cardamoms turn pale brown. Remove from the oven, leaving it on to bake the lamb later.

3. Peel the ginger and garlic, then purée in a hand blender with the roasted spices and a tablespoon of water. Peel the onions and roughly chop these and the tomatoes.

4. Pour 3 tablespoons of the oil into a large pan set over a high heat. The pan should be large enough to hold the lamb shanks in a single layer. When the oil is hot, add the onions and fry for about 10 minutes until they turn a pale caramel colour. Then add the spice paste and stir for another 5 minutes until the onions soften further.

5. Now add the spice powders, the lamb shanks and the tomatoes, and stir like mad for 10 minutes. Add salt to taste; cover the shanks in hot water, place a lid on the pan and leave to cook on a medium heat for 1 hour. Stir from time to time to make sure the ingredients don't get stuck to the bottom of the pan. »

165

6. In the meantime, peel and slice the potatoes into slim straws, place on a baking sheet and coat with the remaining tablespoon of oil. Sprinkle with salt and bake for about 25 minutes, flipping them over midway. Remove from the oven as soon as they are done, to prevent them from going soggy. You could use ready-made oven chips instead, but I think it's far more satisfying to make your own.

7. When the lamb falls away from the bone when probed with a fork, sprinkle over the sugar, the Worcestershire sauce and the apricots. The curry should be rich and thick, so do add a bit of water if it is too dry, or whack up the heat and stir ferociously for 5 minutes if it's too runny.

8. To serve, spoon a lamb shank on to a plate with a serving of chips and Parsi Brown Rice (see the box on page 171). Then lap up all the compliments that come your way.

Murgh Makhani
Butter chicken, mother of the chicken tikka masala

If I had my way, I would ban all sports television from the house. Just watching it makes me feel tired. I don't encourage sports-themed evenings, either. Watching hormonally charged adults yell expletives at a screen while I lovingly cook a full curry for them is hardly entertaining for me.

I gave in for some rugby match that England was a shoo-in to win. The man's three brothers and sister-in-law came over for an evening of Indian food and sporting history. The rare occasion gave me a half-decent reason to unload a large chunk of butter into a curry. Creamy, buttery and tender, the mother of all chicken tikka masalas was duly born in my kitchen. And I didn't have to wait another four years to triumph with this one.

Feeds 10
2kg (4lb 4oz) boneless
  skinless chicken breasts
whole spices
  8 green cardamoms
  16 black peppercorns
  10cm (4in) cinnamon stick
  16 cloves
5cm (2in) root ginger
16 garlic cloves
4 tbsp freshly squeezed
  lemon juice
300g (11oz) natural
  Greek yoghurt
2 tsp kasoori methi
  (dried fenugreek leaves)
1.3kg (3lb) passata
142ml carton of soured
  cream
500g (1lb 2oz) butter
  (you can reduce the
  quantity of butter by up
  to a half, but it will alter
  the flavour of the dish)
salt

1. Preheat the oven to 200°C (400°F), gas mark 6.

2. Cut the chicken into large bite-sized chunks and pile into a mixing bowl. Place the whole spices on a baking sheet and dry-roast for about 30 seconds until you can smell them strongly.

3. Peel the ginger and garlic and whiz together with the roasted spices in a hand blender. Add a little bit of water to get a smooth paste. You could powder the spices separately, but it's far too tiresome.

4. Don't worry if the paste is a little grainy. Add it to the chicken, along with some salt, the lemon juice and 250g (9oz) of yoghurt, and mix well. Leave to tenderise for 2–3 hours in the fridge. When you are ready to eat, preheat the oven again to 200°C (400°F), gas mark 6.

5. Spoon the pieces of chicken into two shallow baking trays and bake for 20 minutes until they are cooked white all the way through. You could also skewer the chicken pieces on to metal or moistened bamboo skewers and stick them on a barbecue, cooking them for 10 minutes on each side. »

6. In the meantime, soak the kasoori methi in 2 tablespoons of hot water. Pour the passata into a large pan set over a medium heat. Mix into it the remaining yoghurt, soured cream and butter, chopped into large chunks. When the butter has fully melted and risen to the surface of the curry, stir in the cooked chicken with all its juices and simmer for 10 minutes, or until the oil floats to the top.

7. Finally, stir in the kasoori methi and its water. Serve immediately with Jeera Pulao (see page 170) and Cobra beer for ultimate satisfaction.

Peshawari Naan
Luxurious naan stuffed with nuts and raisins

Peshawari is the decadent cousin of the plain naan. I tried it the moment I felt at ease with the sight of pale, sticky dough clinging to my fingernails. Best avoided after a fresh manicure and before you need to slip into a tiny dress.

I have three tricks with these naans. First, use some elbow grease when you knead. The longer I spend digging my knuckles into the dough, the softer they invariably are. Second, leave the dough to sit in a warm place. In cold weather, this is the oven on its lowest setting. And finally, don't worry about the filling bursting out or trying to achieve the perfect teardrop shape. Just roll them out any way you can and then stretch them into shape.

Feeds 10
300g (11oz) plain white flour, plus extra for dusting
7g sachet fast-action yeast
1 tsp granulated sugar
1½ tsp salt
1 tbsp nigella seeds
6 tbsp low-fat natural yoghurt
6 tbsp whole milk
2 tbsp oil
10 each of cashew nuts, blanched almonds, pistachio kernels
20 raisins
25g (1oz) butter

1. Follow the instructions for making plain naan (see pages 106–7), up until leaving the dough to sit in a bowl for a second time, for 1 hour in a warm place.

2. At this point, crush all the nuts together roughly in a coffee grinder. Extract the dough from where you left it and punch it down again. Turn the oven on to its highest setting, placing a baking sheet lined with foil on the middle shelf. »

3. Tear the dough into six even balls. Flatten each one on a lightly floured work surface or chopping board and stuff with 3–4 raisins and a tablespoon of the nut mixture. Next, with a flour-dusted rolling pin, roll to about 0.5cm (¼in) thick and stretch into a teardrop shape. Use as little flour as possible and shake off any excess, as this will turn the naan hard in the oven.

4. I would recommend putting no more than two on the baking sheet at one time. They need only 3–4 minutes for brown spots to appear and fluff up. (No need to flip them over during cooking.) Get the next two on and spread the cooked hot naans with butter. To serve, dampen them slightly and microwave for 30 seconds, or in a medium–hot oven for 5 minutes, then drizzle with some chopped nuts fried in butter for a really decadent treat.

RICE IN SPICE

THERE'S NOTHING QUITE AS VERSATILE AS PULAO. CHUCK IN
VEGETABLES AND MEAT AND IT'S A ONE-POT MEAL IN FRONT OF
THE TV. LIGHTLY SPICE IT AND IT'S A WONDERFUL WAY TO QUICKLY
DRESS UP PLAIN OL' RICE FOR A SPECIAL OCCASION.

The key here is to use woody and fragrant whole spices like brown
cardamoms, cinnamon and star anise and to resist the temptation
to stir when the pulao is cooking. I add one-and-a-half times as
much boiling water as rice, both measured in the same builder's
tea mug. That way the rice cooks without going all starchy.
You could always add another half a cup of hot water if
the rice is too al dente for your liking.

WHEN YOU WANT TO GO THAT EXTRA MILE, HERE'S WHAT TO MAKE:
FEEDS 3-4 IN EACH CASE

JEERA PULAO

In a medium pan, sauté 1 brown cardamom, a 2.5cm
(1in) cinnamon stick, 1 star anise and 1 teaspoon of cumin
seeds in 1 tablespoon of hot ghee until sizzling. Add 350g (12oz)
well-rinsed basmati rice, stir until translucent and then add
one-and-a-half times as much hot water as rice. Add salt to
taste, bring to the boil, then lower the heat, cover with a
lid and simmer until the water evaporates and rice is
soft and fluffy.

PARSI BROWN RICE

Fry a 5cm (2in) cinnamon stick, 2 brown cardamoms,
2 bay leaves and 1 teaspoon of granulated sugar in
1 tablespoon of hot oil until sizzling. Then add a sliced
onion and fry until partly golden. Chuck in 350g
(12oz) rinsed basmati rice and proceed as above.

MATTAR PULAO (PULAO WITH PEAS)

Sauté a 5cm (2in) cinnamon stick, 1 bay leaf
and 1 star anise in 2 tablespoons of ghee until sizzling.
Stir in 2 teaspoons of ginger paste, $1/2$ teaspoon of turmeric
powder and 2 mugs of frozen peas. Then stir in 350g
(12oz) rinsed basmati rice and proceed as above.

COCONUT RICE

Cook 350g (12oz) rinsed basmati rice as above, then
fry 1 tablespoon of channa (split yellow) lentils, $1/2$ teaspoon
of mustard seeds, 10 fresh or frozen curry leaves, 2 dried
long red chillies and 2 tablespoons of cashew nuts in
1 tablespoon of oil until golden. Stir the spices into
the cooked rice along with 4 tablespoons of grated
coconut (fresh or frozen), adding salt to taste.

SOME DAYS I AM FULL OF INSPIRED IDEAS. Offering to cater

for my colleague's cocktail party was not one of them. On the face of it, it seemed like a brilliant suggestion. I would cook. My colleagues would eat. I would win the star employee of the month award.

Three grocery trips later, I realised my mistake. Feeding 20 hungry but weight-conscious PR people is tricky on most days. Doing it on a Thursday night at a colleague's house is pushing it. Worse still, my best intentions had turned me into the pre-party office clown. The jokes were on me:

'Chez Mallika ...'

'Looking forward to a Mallika kebab!'

'What? I'm going to Buckingham Balti instead.'

But there was no way out. Expectations grew with every new crack at my catering abilities. The pressure was intense. I had to decide on a glam but comfy outfit (red tights were so in). And a selection of nibbles that would be easy to cook and fill hungry stomachs at the same time.

Party snacks, it seems, are the mainstay of professional chefs and gluttons for punishment only. I am neither. I'd rather eat my toenails than wrap 50 tiger prawns with 50 slices of prosciutto or fashion 50 little kebabs to shallow-fry in batches. The trick for wild parties, I have learnt, is to keep it simple. Bake or grill large quantities instead. Cook a day in advance. And serve food cold. The perfect formula. My crowd-feeding favourites are dishes like Murgh Malai Kebabs, boneless cubes of chicken baked in a double cream, cheese, yoghurt and saffron marinade, and healthy vegetable kebabs spiced with a punchy masala. With two raita-esque dips and strips of ready-made naan, I'm always set to stage the Mallika show.

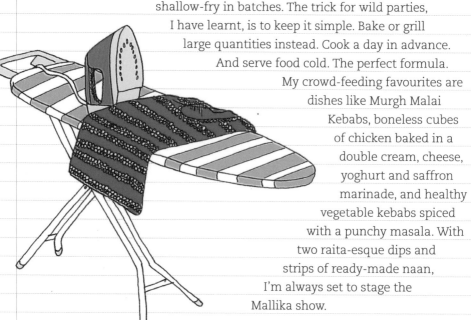

As I was preparing my stuff to strut at the colleague's party, I was gripped with a kebab crisis:

1. NO GREEN BANANAS
I'd have to ditch vegetarian kebabs in favour of spur-of-the-moment lentil and vegetable bites.

2. SOGGY DOUGH
I was more likely to plaster walls with the watery paste I'd just created than fashion 40 little croquettes.

3. ONE HOUR TO PARTY
My nails smelt of ginger. Hair exuded onions. Sequinned vest needed ironing …

I didn't ever want to hear the words 'Madhur', 'Jaffrey' and 'perfect' spoken in the same sentence. Panic-stricken and distraught, I flung half a mug of flour into a mixing bowl, greased two shallow baking trays, spooned in the lentil and vegetable mixture and stuck the whole lot under the grill. With a bloodcurdling 'Honeeeeeeeey!', I drafted the man in to help, while I jumped into the shower, squeezed into skinny jeans, did my makeup and skipped back into the kitchen to quickly cut the mixture into bite-sized pieces.

I arrived at the party a little late, but as cool as my cucumber raita. By this time, it was in full swing. My colleagues had never been happier to see me. I was ushered in with a welcome normally reserved for Olympic gold medallists. One colleague unloaded the platters from me to help serve. Another poured me a glass of chilled wine. While a third heaped generous praise on me.

And mother of all surprises – the Dal Tikkis (as the lentil bites had now been christened) were the biggest hit of the evening! Leaning casually over the bookcase, glass of vino in one hand, I lapped up the attention, claiming they had been *ridiculously simple* to make from a recipe I had been using for *years*. Party trick completed, I promptly got drunk and passed out. Perfection. In my world anyway.

Dal Tikkis
Grilled lentil bites spiced with ginger and cinnamon

Tikkis are actually meant to be round and flat, like mini burgers. But these tray-grilled ones are much easier to get ready for a large group of people. I've made these several times. Most notably, for a camera crew during one of my failed attempts to knock the socks off the nation on TV. Still, they seemed to enjoy these spicy lentil bites.

The 'dough' for this needs to be as dry as possible to help you mould it. I tend to add enough water to cover the lentils in the pan, and extra only if they start hissing and spitting everywhere. The benefit of grilling also means any unnecessary moisture will get zapped out of it and you'll hardly need any oil, either.

Serves 20
Vegetarian
8cm (3in) root ginger
whole spices
  8 cloves
  5cm (2in) cinnamon stick
  4 bay leaves
  1 tsp black peppercorns
250g (9oz) channa
  (split yellow) lentils
2 medium onions
4 large carrots
6 large potatoes
125g (4½oz) fresh
  coriander, roughly chopped
75g (3oz) plain four
2 tbsp oil
salt

1. Peel the ginger and purée in a blender with the whole spices and a tablespoon of warm water to form a smooth paste. Wash the lentils thoroughly under a cold tap until the water runs clean, and peel and roughly chop the onions. Then peel and cut the carrots and potatoes into bite-sized chunks.

2. Place the lentils in a large pan, adding the same amount of water as lentils, the masala paste and the chopped vegetables. Bring to a gentle boil and cook for 20 minutes until the vegetables are soft and you can squish the lentil pieces easily. You want them to soften but not disintegrate completely into a dal.

3. Remove from the heat and drain the mixture of any water that may remain. Mix in the fresh coriander, flour and salt to taste, and mash well until you get a semi-smooth dough. If the dough is too watery, you could mix in a quarter cup of plain white flour.

4. Preheat the grill to high. Line a shallow baking tray with foil and grease lightly with 1 tablespoon of the oil. Spoon the mixture into the baking tray and smooth the top to make an even layer. »

5. Grill for 15 minutes on one side. Then cover the tray with a wire rack, flip the dough over, add the other tablespoon of oil to the tray and then place the dough back in to cook on the other side for a further 15 minutes. This is easier than it sounds, with the added benefit that you can simply piece back any bits of the mixture that fall out.

6. Leave the whole lot to cool in the tray, cutting into bite-sized nibbles when festivities are about to commence. Stack them on a plate and serve with tomato ketchup spiked with chilli powder.

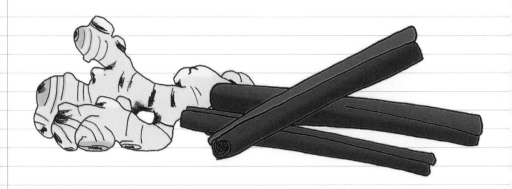

Murgh Malai Kebabs
Melt-in-the-mouth creamy chicken kebabs

Sitting under the whirring fans of the sports and leisure centre at Saturday Club in the heat of a Kolkata winter, I wondered for years how they got their chicken breast kebabs so tender. My attempts to cook with the same parts of the bird invariably ended up as small inedible rocks that tasted remarkably like flavoured rubber.

The secret, I have learnt since, is to soften the meat with a tenderiser. This white powder comes packaged like any other masala and is made up of papain, a papaya enzyme, and salt. Mix a little into your marinade and even chicken breast chunks will melt in the mouth.

Serves 20

15cm (6in) root ginger
cloves of 1 garlic bulb
6 fresh green finger chillies
3kg (6½lb) skinless boneless
  chicken breasts
500g (1lb 2oz) natural
  Greek yoghurt
600ml (1 pint) double cream
300g (11oz) cream cheese
½ nutmeg
1 tsp saffron
3 tsp meat tenderiser
3 tbsp oil, plus extra
  for greasing
salt

20 bamboo skewers (or
metal if using a barbecue)

1. Peel the ginger and garlic and purée with the green finger chillies and oil in a blender or food processor. Cut the chicken into chunks slightly larger than bite-sized, bearing in mind that they will shrink as they cook.

2. In a large mixing bowl, mix together the ginger and chilli paste with all the remaining ingredients apart from the chicken, adding salt to taste. Taste it to make sure the marinade is pungent, as it will lose some of its strong flavour when cooked.

3. Next add the chicken, stirring so that it is coated evenly with the marinade. Cover with cling film and leave it for at least 2 hours in the fridge, or overnight if possible. I did this on the Tuesday to save preparation time on the Wednesday before the party.

4. Just before you need the kebabs, preheat the oven to 200°C (400°F), gas mark 6. Lightly oil three baking trays.

5. Place the chicken pieces on the trays, cooking these in two batches for about 20 minutes each. You may have to rotate the trays to make sure each of them gets a spell in the hottest part of the oven (the top). Alternatively, » you could always thread them on to metal or moistened bamboo skewers and barbecue them for 10 minutes on each side.

6. When cooked, the chicken will be cooked through and speckled with dark brown spots on their surface. Pile them up on a platter and serve with Dhaniya Pudina Chutney (see pages 120–1).

Vodka Chilli Cocktails
Mother's special for those who dare

This drink isn't for the faint-hearted. Which is why, I suspect, my mother gave it to her mother every Sunday. My father gleefully stirred it in a tall glass and watched peacefully as his mother-in-law tottered off to bed, uncharacteristically subdued, steam emanating from her ears.

The closest I've come to these in London is the chilli 'n' chocolate cocktails served in the cocktail lounges of trendy Shoreditch, deep in the bowels of Brick Lane. At £10 a glass, they're not cheap. But in such decadent places, with thick velvet curtains, antique bric-a-brac and low lighting, they are worth experiencing. Try my mother's version at home on its own, or with a spicy curry if you dare.

Serves 2
4 fresh green finger chillies
½ tsp kala namak
  (black rock salt)
½ tsp freshly ground
  black pepper
2 single shots of vodka
4–6 ice cubes
1 x 350ml can of lemonade
2 slices of lime, to serve

2 Martini glasses

1. Make a 2cm (¾in) slit along the thickest part of each chilli, taking care not to cut right through. In a small cup, mix together the salt and pepper. With the tip of your knife, stuff the chilli slits with the salt and pepper mix.

2. Now measure a shot of vodka into each Martini glass and place two chillies in each. Leave to soak for at least 10 minutes, while you crush the ice. Then add a handful of crushed ice to each glass, top with lemonade and a sprinkle of any remaining salt and pepper. Decorate with a slice of lime to serve.

ALL ABOUT CHILLIES

CHILLIES ARE THE LIFE AND SOUL OF A HEARTY INDIAN MEAL.
YOU DON'T HAVE TO OVERDO IT UNTIL SMOKE COMES OUT OF YOUR EARS,
BUT WITHOUT A TOUCH OF CHILLI, DISHES SEEM INCOMPLETE.
LIKE LATTE WITHOUT A SPRINKLING OF CHOCOLATE POWDER
OR POTATO WEDGES WITHOUT KETCHUP.

There is great variety in the chillies used in Indian recipes.
Fresh, red or green, dried, whole or powdered. Not only do they
add the fire we love them for, but also flavour in bucketloads.
Just remember we don't deseed them. Be bold yourself and use the
whole lot instead. Here's my run-down of the top of the crop:

GREEN FINGER CHILLIES

Slim and potent, these chillies have a lovely fresh flavour
and a sharp bite. You can buy them in packets or loose from
ethnic shops. Green finger chillies are often slit/chopped
and added to dishes. In Kolkata, each morsel of food is
accompanied by a little bite of a fresh finger chilli. These
chillies are not the same as the milder and less flavoursome
green and red chillies available widely in supermarkets.
If finger chillies are unavailable, keep a bottle of
ethnic store-bought, ready-minced ones handy.

DRIED WHOLE RED CHILLIES

There are two types. One looks like a finger chilli,
only fatter and red. The other is about 1cm ($\frac{1}{2}$ in) long
and more potent. They are often fried in oil as a tadka before
being added to the dish where their flavour seeps into
the sizzling hot oil or ghee. I use the longer ones,
as they're easier to fish out and less lethal if
you bite into one accidentally.

CHILLI POWDER

Although sold in varying degrees of strength,
from 'mild' to 'extra-hot', this stuff is more potent
than anything listed above. It has a propensity to set ears
buzzing, tongues tingling and can upset the stomach.
A lot of takeaway cuisine is spiced with chilli powder.
Used in moderation, it adds a lovely red glow and sharp
flavour to dishes without setting anything on fire.

THE RULE OF THUMB WITH CHILLIES IS TO WORK OUT HOW MUCH YOU
CAN TOLERATE AND THEN ADD JUST A LITTLE BIT MORE FOR THAT EXTRA
BITE. MY DAD, FOR EXAMPLE, COOKS A MEAT DISH THAT USES A KILO
OF LAMB AND A KILO OF THE LITTLE DRIED RED CHILLIES. IT PUSHES
HIS CHILLI THRESHOLD SLIGHTLY BUT JUST ABOUT BLOWS
ANYONE ELSE'S THROUGH THE ROOF.

ONE OTHER THING TO REMEMBER IS THAT INDIAN FOOD
WAS NEVER MEANT TO BE SEARINGLY HOT. JUST LIKE ANY
OTHER CUISINE, IT'S THE TASTE THAT MATTERS, WHICH
CAN BE DISGUISED BY TOO MUCH CHILLI.

INDIAN PARTY FOOD FOR CHEATS

There are parties, and then there are really wild parties. The ones where you honestly can't give a toss about making sure everyone is fed. When lighting, iTunes and a well-stocked bar are infinitely more important than Dal Tikkis, which might end up splattered on the wall anyway, along with a spray of Bordeaux. These rare occasions offer just a small window of opportunity to line everyone's tummies before the carnage ensues. Don't waste your time – serve the cheats' treats listed opposite to impress your guests, if only momentarily.

VINDALOO SAUSAGES

Cocktail sausages marinated for 2 hours in pork vindaloo masala and grilled as per pack instructions. Reheat in the microwave or a medium oven before serving. Store-bought spicy mango chutney makes a great glaze to use as an option.

JEERA ALOO

Parboiled new potatoes tossed in sizzling cumin seeds, cumin, coriander and chilli powder. Serve cold with toothpicks.

CHUTNEY ALOO

Boiled new potatoes smothered with coriander and mint chutney (see pages 120-1). Toothpicks a must here.

CORIANDER AND MINT RAITA

Fresh coriander and mint stirred into Greek yoghurt. Or any raita made with thick Greek yoghurt (see the box on pages 114-5). Served with strips of ready-made naan.

6.

FOOD FOR FEELING BETTER

Pick-me-ups for all your woes

Miss Masala.

TECHNICALLY, IT SHOULD HAVE BEEN A DAY when dreams

came true. The Christmas sales had started. I couldn't wait to bag some bargains during my shopping extravaganza. Those custom-fitted knee-high boots. That must-have leather bomber. The perfectly impractical angora overcoat. All purchased with debit cards only, since a run-in with irate bankers nearly a decade ago over the state of my credit cards.

Discovering London's high street was a life-changing experience. Until recently, the basement of Austin Reed was my pinnacle of high fashion. Too many years in the corporate world had skewed my perspective slightly. Anything grey, pin-striped, with shoulder pads was achingly desirable. That was weekday clothing, of course. Weekends, I limited myself to casuals purchased at Gap or Benetton. With Zara providing the occasional injection of contemporary style, I teetered on the brink of fashion self-destruction like the average Trinny and Susannah victim.

Since starting my blog, I've paid more attention to Le Look. The man's fashion stylist colleague was coerced into giving me crucial pointers like: 'Show those legs off, darling.' Seasonal essentials are purchased routinely from the high street. With more pointless purchases reserved for sales bonanzas.

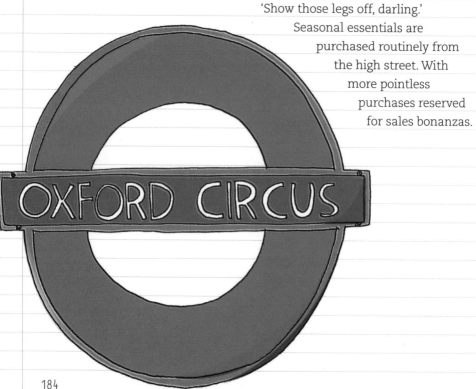

I could barely conceal my excitement as I charged down to Oxford Street, that infamous central London hub of crazed consumerism. The trains were heaving. It was an early premonition of the madness that was to come. Still, I emerged from Oxford Circus tube full of beans. And then I spotted the rest of south-east England. Out to fill the same imaginary holes in their wardrobes.

Things quickly disintegrated. Within minutes, a pushchair nearly ran me over. Preoccupied teenagers meandered into me. The first retail emporium on my list resembled a Third World sweatshop – clothes in piles, people everywhere and air quality that would have the Department of Health running for cover. Worse still, a long queue for the fitting room snaked through the mess. What was the point anyway? A gangly student had just appropriated the last bomber in my size from under my nose.

C'est la vie … I took a sideways detour into Regent Street. Home of the slightly more upmarket high street. The shops were less busy. But dangerously close to corporate Britain. I saw Austin Reed and baulked. If I gave in now, there would be no turning back. I ran into a high-street favourite. Bought a white leather bag, an armload of party tops in shiny polyester and headed home towards a stiff drink, clutching an oversize bag emblazoned with S-A-L-E.

The man was glued to the TV as I entered the flat. A fashion and beauty photographer, he is my unofficial style guru and fiercest fashion critic. I slid past him and shoved the bag inside the wardrobe. He immediately smelt a rat.

'Helloooo … what did you buy?'

'Nothing.'

'You were out for three hours?'

'There wasn't much in the shops.'

'You must have bought something?'

Blast.

Note to myself: practice innocent, lying tone.

I fished the bag out of the wardrobe and reluctantly put my purchases on display.

'You'll only use that white leather bag twice before it's dirt grey and donated to Oxfam.'

I launched a fierce protest. It failed.

'You don't need these party tops.'

'They were only £10 each,' I defended myself.

'And they look it!'

I admitted defeat. The goodies went back into the bag. They would be returned to the store in due course.

The events of the day had left me a little bit low. I thought about ringing the Japanese take-away and quickly decided against it. Why, when spices are well known for their mood-enhancing and therapeutic properties? Whole spices like bay leaves, cardamoms, cinnamon and cloves are stimulants with heating properties. Coriander and cumin have the ability to cool and aid digestion. And eating hot chillies releases feel-good endorphins and burns the tongue, temporarily distracting from other niggling worries.

Apart from Indian spices, give me a sharp knife, sturdy chopping board and a few onions to vent my frustrations at the end of a long day. Imagine a head on the block and that's about as much visualisation technique required for miraculous recovery. More seriously, though, I suspect that the real reason Indian food is so therapeutic is because I really have to focus when cooking it. When feeling down in the dumps, just roll up your sleeves, build an aroma- and colour-steeped assembly line, and lovingly create your very own mood-lifting meal.

IT'S OFFICIAL.
SPICES CAN MAKE YOU FEEL BETTER!

	DIGESTIVE	DECONGESTANT	ANTI-INFLAMMATORY	ANTIOXIDANT	APHRODISIAC	ANTISEPTIC
ASAFOETIDA	🐘		🐘	🐘		
BAY LEAVES						
CARDAMOM	🐘	🐘			🐘	
CHILLIES	🐘	🐘	🐘			
CINNAMON	🐘		🐘			
CLOVES			🐘		🐘	🐘
CORIANDER	🐘		🐘			
CUMIN	🐘					
TURMERIC	🐘		🐘	🐘		🐘

Parathas: Aloo, Gajar and Mooli

Three ways with moreish stuffed flatbreads

My opinion of kneading is well documented. I rank it as one of my most hated activities, second only to standing naked in a blizzard on one leg. But on rainy or miserable days, stuffed parathas are really worth getting dough all over clothes, hair and the kitchen floor. You can use the sorry contents of your fridge to create the most moreish and comforting meal in one.

Parathas can be stuffed with a number of different spiced fillings, from cauliflower and peas to keema. But my favourites are the ones my nani brought with her from her family home in Delhi to our Kolkata household – filled with carrot, potato or radish.

Makes 4 stuffed parathas
Vegetarian

For the parathas
4 tbsp natural Greek yoghurt
250g (9oz) strong wholemeal or chappati flour, plus extra for dusting
1 tsp salt
4 tbsp oil

For fillings, see opposite page

1. First make the dough. Warm the yoghurt in a small pan on the hob or in the microwave on high for 30 seconds. It must be warm (or at room temperature) to help break the flour down and make it soft.

2. Sift the flour and salt into a medium-sized mixing bowl, then mix in the yoghurt a half at a time. Go in with one hand and mix it well until the mixture resembles biscuit crumbs. You want to keep breaking it down like this when you add the rest of the yoghurt. Then add a little hot water, a spoonful at a time, punching the dough with your knuckles on every side until you get a smooth mix that doesn't stick to your fingers.

3. If it sticks to your fingers, you've added too much water, so just chuck in a bit more flour. (This isn't as problematic as it sounds.) Keep kneading or punching the dough, backwards and forwards, for at least 5 minutes. The more you beat it, the softer it'll be when it's cooked.

4. Cover with a clean, damp tea towel and set aside while you make one of the stuffings. »

Select one of the following fillings:

For the aloo (potato) filling
2 medium potatoes
1 small onion
2 fresh green finger chillies
1 tsp freshly squeezed
  lime juice
2 tbsp chopped fresh
  coriander
salt

For the gajar (carrot) filling
4 small carrots
2 tsp freshly squeezed
  lime juice
½ tsp chilli powder
salt

For the mooli (radish) filling
0.5cm (¼ in) root ginger
8 small radishes
1 fresh green finger chilli
2 tbsp chopped fresh
  coriander
salt

5. For the aloo stuffing, peel and quarter the potatoes, then either microwave on high for about 5 minutes with 2 tablespoons of hot water or boil for 15–20 minutes in a small pan on the hob. Meanwhile, peel and finely chop the onion and slice up the chillies. Drain and mash the potatoes, then mix with all the other stuffing ingredients, adding salt to taste.

6. For the carrot stuffing, peel and grate the carrots and mix with the remaining ingredients, adding salt to taste. Then either microwave for 2 minutes on high or sauté in a small pan over a high heat for 2 minutes.

7. For the radish stuffing, peel the ginger, then finely chop along with the radishes and chilli. Mix with the coriander, add salt to taste and heat as in step 6.

8. Next, uncover the dough mix and, using the palms of your hands, shape it into a thick sausage and break into four equal parts. Sprinkle a clean work surface or large chopping board with flour, then roll one of the dough lumps into a ball and flatten with a rolling pin into a disc the size of a small saucer.

9. Spoon 2 teaspoons of your choice of filling into the centre and bring the edges together like a sack to enclose the filling, pinching the edges together with your fingers to seal them. Dust with flour, then carefully flatten and roll it out into a disc about 0.5cm (¼in) thick. Don't worry if the filling starts oozing out. This is the way it's meant to be. Repeat with other dough balls.

10. Now, pour 1 tablespoon of the oil into a tawa or large frying pan set over a high heat. When the oil is sizzling, place a stuffed paratha on top and fry for 2 minutes on each side until dark brown spots appear. If the oil dries up, just drizzle a tiny bit more into the pan, around the edges of the paratha.

11. Repeat until you have four, devilishly soft, moreishly tasty parathas. As you make them, wrap them in foil or a clean towel to keep them warm or serve them individually hot off the tawa. They are delicious with pickle and a large dollop of natural yoghurt.

Maacher Cutlets
Healthy baked masala-battered fish fillets

Attending a friend's dinner party is always a joy. I sit around doing little. Offering my views on critical world issues, like sweatshops and custom-made boots. Meanwhile, my poor friend slaves away to get a three-course dinner on to the immaculately laid table on time.

Too much eating out, however, and I need a simple but reassuringly fiddly recipe to reinstate myself in the kitchen again. Spicy, breaded fish fillets, Maacher Cutlets are one of those recipes that also help take the mind off other matters. Although traditionally deep-fried, the fillets are obligatorily grilled in my kitchen. Only after I've changed into a comfy pair of shorts, taken one last look at my fluorescent manicured fingernails and plunged into an assembly line of fish marinade and coatings.

Feeds 2
1cm (½in) root ginger
3 garlic cloves
1 large onion
2 fresh green finger chillies
4 small, skinless white fish fillets (basa, cod and plaice work well), all bones removed (about 275g/10oz in total)
2–3 tbsp oil
1 egg
100g (3½oz) plain flour
4 tbsp ready-made golden breadcrumbs
salt
2 lemon wedges, to serve

1. Peel the ginger and garlic and peel and roughly chop the onion. In a blender or food processor, purée these with the chillies, adding salt to taste. Coat each fillet on both sides with this marinade and leave to sit on a covered plate.

2. Now, establish your assembly line. First, turn the grill on to high. Next, line a baking tray with foil and spread the oil over it. In a shallow bowl, beat the egg, then place the flour on one plate and the breadcrumbs on another.

3. Line up the flour, egg, breadcrumbs and baking tray near the grill. Dip each side of a marinated fish fillet into the flour, patting to coat evenly so no onion mixture is exposed. Then dip in the egg and finally the breadcrumbs. As each fillet is fully coated, lay it on the baking tray.

4. Repeat this process until all the fish fillets have been coated. Then grill for 10 minutes on each side, until you have four golden brown and crisp Maacher Cutlets.

5. Serve this with the lemon wedges, a summer salad and some Tamatar Chutney (see page 120) for a quirky but healthy TV meal.

I ARRIVED HOME ONE EVENING to find the man sprawled across

the couch. Toilet paper wedged into his nostrils. Room lighting abysmally low.
The TV tuned into a quiz show. This was man flu. The common cold dressed
as worst-grade pneumonia.

It couldn't have been more ill timed. We were due to go food shopping. But
trips in the luxury of our Knight Rider were temporarily out of the question.
I can't drive. Neither can any of the women in my family. The Basu sisters
were not built to drive

The last time I tried, the instructor shouted 'Are you stupid!' at me as
I drove full speed through a red light. A few days earlier, he claimed I had
'serious potential' to be driving a sports car into the sunset. Undeterred by
his change of heart, I insisted on showing off my newly honed talent and
drove our beast straight into a parked lime green Polo on our street. The only
wheels I've manoeuvred since are the ones on a shopping trolley. And even
that was out of the question now with my ailing man.

I needed to cure him, fast. There was only one thing that would work.
Lashings of focused attention from loving and dutiful *moi*, served with a large
spoonful of spicy curry on brown basmati rice. That, and hot honey and
lemon drinks. Three days of undivided attention later, the man
had recovered. The fridge was left with the meagre
contents of half-consumed condiments and
shrivelled green chillies.

It was time to put our blessed union through
the ultimate test – a supermarket trip. The man
collected me from work and we headed to an
enormous supermarket to restock for the
days ahead. I had planned to make a
detailed shopping list. Put the many
cookbooks I own to good use by selecting
seasonal recipes with overlapping
ingredients and then buying them all in
an organised fashion. Forgetting I had
planned and failed to be organised
throughout my entire adult life.

We drove down to the behemoth and
trailed round it. On empty stomachs.

Tired from the day's events. And with not a clue about what we were looking for. The three essential ingredients for domestic meltdown. I briefly ignored this eventuality. The trip started with mild bickering about sell-by dates and yoghurt brands. As I turned the herb corner, I spotted bags of new Indian ingredients. Curry leaves? Okra? Loose green finger chillies? Aisle 2? Eternal bliss!

I lingered, lovingly sniffing each pack of curry leaves before selecting 'the one' and placing it in our trolley. A silly smile crept on to my face and stayed there. By this time, I had thoroughly tested the man's patience. He proceeded to disappear with the shopping trolley. Loaded a ready-roasted battery chicken and promotional 24-pack beer carton into it. While I rushed round the aisles trying to locate him, a tower of supplies wedged in my arms.

We made it to the checkout with a trolley piled high. The assistant lifted the polythene bag filled with chillies and shot us a suspicious look.

'Where d'you get these?'

From a market stall in sunny Kerala. 'From Aisle 2,' I replied politely.

'I never seen 'em before.'

'They're green chillies from your ethnic vegetables section.'

She drew them close to her and took a deep sniff.

This was turning into a scene from *Sesame Street* …

Her colleague decided to help.

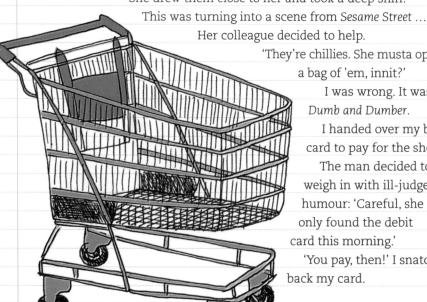

'They're chillies. She musta opened a bag of 'em, innit?'

I was wrong. It was *Dumb and Dumber*.

I handed over my bank card to pay for the shopping. The man decided to weigh in with ill-judged humour: 'Careful, she only found the debit card this morning.'

'You pay, then!' I snatched back my card.

We proceeded to fight at the checkout about whose turn it was to pack and/or pay. Then arrived home with half the essentials missing.

Men. I could go on forever. After all, I haven't been single since I turned 14. Most of my relationships have overlapped, with dramatic love triangles that would put the plot of an average Indian sitcom to shame. A serial monogamist, I have learnt to cope with the trials and tribulations of long-term relationships in my own special way: selective hearing, separate bank accounts and loads of personal space. It seems to be working. Which, of course, qualifies me as a fountain of infinite bloke wisdom.

We were still arguing about who should unpack the shopping when the telephone rang. It was my friend, with a man crisis. Her love interest had seemed okay at first. But quickly exposed himself as a less than desirable specimen for long-term investment. Turns out she was now understandably out of love with him. This sort of situation was my forte. I don't do sympathy. So I launched into a comforting, positive and empowering speech intended to banish her feelings of hopelessness:

'I never liked him anyway.'

'He seemed so nice, so loving.'

'Rubbish. There was always something remiss under that likeable front.'

'What's wrong with me? Why me?'

'Nothing's wrong with you. You just have terrible taste in men. That's all.'

'I am going to be single for ever.' (Tears on the other end of the phone.)

'Of course not. There are plenty more fish in the sea. Can I sign you up to mysinglefriend.com? Puh-lease?'

We agree to meet at a wine bar in two days to discuss the matter in more detail. I make her promise not to do anything she might regret in the meantime. Like telephone him and express her undying love. Or sleep with a colleague/the plumber/other unsuitable interim option. And then I turn my attention back to the shopping splayed all over the kitchen.

The pantry essentials had been flung willy-nilly into the kitchen cupboards. Half-emptied supermarket bags were strewn all over the dining table. The man was comfortably positioned in front of the *Top Gear* repeat, bottle of beer in one hand, remote control in the other. 'You can't live with them, you can't live without,' I muttered to myself. I extracted a chopping board. One large onion. And got to work on a comforting Khichdi for just the two of us.

Khichdi

Rice cooked with sizzling spices
and split red lentils

At its most basic, Khichdi (pronounced 'kich-ree' and
a forerunner of kedgeree) is recovery food. Cooked with
barely any spices compared with the average curry, it soothes,
comforts and cures at the same time. There are a hundred different ways
to make this. But I love this version I discovered in the NIAW Cookbook and
taught myself to cook in the early days.

    This is my favourite pick-me-up on rough days. Tastes superb with papads,
pickle and natural yoghurt. And washes down really well with a stiff drink.
'Nuff said. Enjoy.

Feeds 4

Vegetarian
150g (5oz) basmati rice
75g (3oz) masoor
  (split red) lentils
1 large onion
1 tbsp oil
2.5cm (1in) cinnamon stick
4 cloves
4 green cardamoms
1 bay leaf
1 tsp cumin seeds
½ tsp turmeric powder
1 tsp salt
1 handful of prepared raw
  vegetables, such as diced
  carrots or potatoes,
  cauliflower florets or peas
  (optional)

1. Wash the rice and lentils thoroughly under a cold
tap in the same sieve. While they are draining, peel and
finely slice the onion.

2. Pour the oil into a medium pan set over a high heat
and, when hot, chuck in the cinnamon, cloves,
cardamoms and bay leaf. When the bay leaf starts
turning brown, after just a few seconds, add the cumin
seeds and let them sizzle up for a few more seconds.

3. Add the onion and fry for about 10 minutes until
it starts turning a caramel colour. Mix in the turmeric
and give the masala a good stir. Now tip in the rice
and lentils, and fry for 1 minute, stirring to coat them
evenly in the masala, then add the salt.

4. Lower the heat to medium, add four times as much hot water as rice and
lentils and chuck in the prepared vegetables (if using). Cover with a lid and
leave to cook for 20 minutes, stirring every 5 minutes, until the lentils lose
their shape and the rice is tender. Khichdi should have a runny consistency
like risotto.

Doi Maach

Monkfish lightly stewed in yoghurt and whole spices

Bengalis are famous fish eaters. I never quite inherited this fine cultural trait, however. The sight of a fish head floating in dal or sautéed with vegetables was enough to miraculously cure my myopia without having to dive into the dish.

Even so, a handful of fish curries have worthily made it into my everyday cooking repertoire. Like this one – a light and delicately spiced stew with boneless fish fillets. I use monkfish because it is easy to find in the shops, but for a real authentic touch, look out for rohu or rui fillets at ethnic fishmongers.

Feeds 4

4 monkfish tails, halved
  widthways
½ tsp turmeric powder
1 tsp chilli powder
1 tsp salt
2 medium onions
2.5cm (1in) root ginger
2 tbsp sunflower oil
1 tbsp mustard oil
1 tsp granulated sugar
whole spices
  2 bay leaves
  4 green cardamoms
  4 cloves
  2.5cm (1in) cinnamon stick
500g (1lb 2oz) natural
  Greek yoghurt
2 fresh green finger chillies
1 tbsp raisins

1. Wash the fish well and dab dry on kitchen paper, then place in a large mixing bowl. Add the turmeric and chilli powders and the salt and leave to marinate.

2. Peel the onions and finely slice one. Peel the ginger, then roughly chop with the remaining onion and purée with a hand blender.

3. Pour the sunflower oil into a large, heavy-bottomed, non-stick frying pan set over a high heat. When the oil starts sizzling, fry the fish pieces gently for 2–3 minutes on each side until pale brown and well sealed. Then remove with a slotted spoon and place back in the mixing bowl. You can omit this step entirely but it works wonders to seal in flavours and keep the fish intact.

4. Next, add the mustard oil to the pan, still on a high heat. When the oil starts sizzling, add the sugar. When it caramelises, chuck in the whole spices and, after 5 seconds, the onions and ginger.

5. Fry this on a high heat, stirring like a maniac, until the onions turn pale caramel. You will need to keep adding water, 2 tablespoons at a time, to »

prevent the mixture from sticking to the bottom of the pan. This will take a good 20 minutes to cook; don't give up too early, or the dish will taste raw at the end.

6. When the onion stops smelling raw and pungent and takes on a golden hue, reduce the heat to low for 2 minutes. Stir in the yoghurt and the green finger chillies and simmer for 10 minutes until the curry is an even pale gold in colour.

7. Finally, lower the fish pieces into the curry and sprinkle in the raisins. Leave to simmer for 10 minutes until oil emerges through little pores in the curry. You should have just enough thick curry to coat the fillets. Serve with rice cooked with a tablespoon of ghee for a real taste of Bengal.

FISHY BUSINESS

BUYING FISH DOES NOT COME NATURALLY TO ME.

I've tried everything - Harrods Food Hall, the farmers'
market, the supermarket fish counter. I stand there, quivering
in my knee-high boots. Demanding fish that doesn't smell or
taste fishy and won't fall apart in a curry. While ignoring
the evil looks I'm receiving from the behind the counter
and the long queue forming behind me.

When cooking with fish, I gravitate towards what's pre-cleaned,
filleted and preferably pre-packed. Cod, plaice and pomfret
fillets work well for marinated steamed or oven-cooked dishes.
Other, meatier white varieties are better for curry, such as
monkfish, tilapia and sea bass. When in doubt, just bite the
bullet and ask the fishmonger.

Skin or no skin depends entirely upon you and the recipe
in question. Also, while you would think the word 'boneless'
actually stands for something, it doesn't guarantee your
fillets will be free of the annoying things. Give the
fish a good wash under a cold tap before you proceed
with the recipe.

Masala Chai
A hot spiced cuppa and a giant hug in a mug

When the words chai tea appeared in coffee shops around here, it got me thinking of the genuine article, which for years I have been enjoying out of little disposable terracotta mugs back in India. I gave up fags, coffee, normal tea and coped just fine. But a frothy spiced cuppa on crisp or sickly days is just too divine to decline.

There are two ways to make this at home. I brew the spices whole with the milk. But you could also make a masala chai powder using your coffee grinder for several uses. Just add 1 teaspoon to the milk before you boil it. The trick is to always use whole milk and add as much sugar as you can possibly stomach. The result is aromatic, potent and worth every second. A proper hug in a mug when it's needed most.

Serves 2
Vegetarian
whole spices
  10 green cardamoms
  5cm (2in) cinnamon stick
  4 black peppercorns
2.5cm (1in) root ginger
600ml (1 pint) whole milk
2 heaped tsp granulated
  sugar
2 teabags of Assam
  or other strong tea

1. Crush the whole spices roughly, using the flat side of a knife, and peel and slice the ginger. Add to a medium pan along with the milk and bring to a gentle boil. Alternatively, grind the spices into a fine powder in a coffee grinder and add a teaspoon of it to the boiling milk and ginger.

2. Cook for about 5 minutes, stirring all the time, until the milk turns a pale cream colour and the spices smell strongly fragrant. Next, mix in the sugar and the teabags and keep bubbling for another minute until the tea takes on a rich, dark colour.

3. Strain into two cups, pouring from as high as you can manage to get a frothy head on each drink, then sit back, take a sip and feel your troubles melt away.

I HAD A BAD FEELING that Friday. Desks normally cluttered with

M&S Percy Pigs and fat-free rice cakes now housed cartons of Lemsip, sacks of satsumas and family-size boxes of tissues. The gobby colleague across from me opened his mouth from time to time to let out the most almighty, unprotected sneeze. I resisted the urge to duck for cover and kick him under the table as I felt the germ particles disperse around us.

Damn the modern-day work culture. My immune system was under serious pressure, just as my social life was about to take a positive step towards world music. My Norwegian-Scottish girlfriend had a big night out planned. My favourite culture vulture, the leggy brunette has a nose for sniffing out the best fringe theatre, dance performances and live concerts in town. That's when she's not devising international strategies for her superiors, baking cupcakes or planning exotic holidays.

I went home looking forward to Saturday night's Orishas gig. An exiled boy band from Castro land, these gyrating, hip-thrusting Latino rappers make the stereotypical retired Cuban musicians look like a granddads' convention. Culture vulture had discovered a little gem amidst the myriad offerings of La Linea, the annual Latin American music festival on the South Bank. And I was determined to enjoy every moment of it.

The weekend finally arrived. As if by magic, so did a cold. Distraught and panic-stricken, I telephoned Kolkata. Mother showered me with sympathy. Asked me if I was wearing enough woollens? Getting enough vitamin C? Brushing my teeth? I didn't need maternal admonitions! I needed age-old Indian miracle remedies for the common cold! Mother finally suggested honey and lemon, a good book and the homeopathy remedy Bryonia 30. Also, a quiet, reflective weekend: 'Being ill is God's way of telling you to slow down.'

I quietly reflected my fate. Culture vulture was depending on me to shake my booty. I couldn't let her and the rest of the group down. So I popped paracetamol and made my way to the Royal Festival Hall. Where I momentarily forgave the germ-ridden colleague, drank red wine and danced furiously to the eclectic hip-hop/salsa/rap thrust in our faces by two-and-a-half cute Cubans.

The limp home was just the beginning. By Sunday morning, my nostrils flared to the size of base drums. My nose had lost its sense of purpose.

My voice reduced to a hoarse whisper. The only sensation I had left was a buzzing in my ears from the oversized speakers. I needed a rescue operation that would charge through me, airlifting my scattered senses back to where they belonged.

Unsurprisingly, Indian food is replete with recipes guaranteed to make you feel better. Light chicken dishes such as Jeera Chicken are healthy and full of the amino acids that produce happy hormones. That's for when I'm feeling fat, old or pre-menstrual. Yoghurt and curry leaves soothe and aid digestion – perfect for tummy bugs. For my cold, I chose Rasam. This potent spicy and sour soup hails from south India. But it is famously enjoyed all across the country. People swear by its ability to banish even the most dastardly colds by setting the taste buds alight and rebooting the mind.

The most basic rasam is the one that uses just tamarind water. I opted for a more substantial Tomato Rasam, the kind I drank in 'south Indian' restaurants back home. I roasted the ten dried whole red chillies required by the recipe. As they expelled their sharp, pungent kick into the kitchen, my head cleared up. By the time I had completed the soup, I could actually taste and smell it! I eagerly wrote about the wondrous concoction on my blog and kept drinking it until I temporarily paralysed my taste buds.

Then, as if by magic, an angel of mercy appeared. In the form of fellow blogger Sia of the Monsoon Spice blog. Forget a bucketload of sympathy; this woman e-mailed me her amma (or mother's) recipe for Pepper Rasam. I dived into yet another tried and tested recipe for the soup. Four cups of her stuff and I could feel the groove coming back. I went back to work with barely a sniffle or cough.

By the end of that week, I was looking for another big Saturday night. I was fully germ-free and ready for crazy dance moves, lots of gin and the friend's big 3-0. I was ready to live up to my own expectations.

MOTHER'S MIRACLE CURES

When my busy schedule of work deadlines, evenings out and
all-day shopping bonanzas are forced by illness to a grinding
halt, there is one person I turn to in desperation.

MOTHER

Mother has spent hours of her life lying prostrate in bed,
with salad ingredients on her face, minced leaves in her hair
and a cup of homemade curative brew by her side. Nothing upsets
her karma quite like her daughters in distress. And little
pleases her more than being requested to pass on her infinite
wisdom and miracle cures to us, such as:

FRESH GINGER AND BLACK PEPPER TEA to unblock sinuses.

POUNDED-FENNEL-SEED TEA to aid digestion.

LEMON JUICE FACE-PACK to even out a dodgy suntan.

POTATO- OR CUCUMBER-JUICE-SOAKED COTTON PADS on the eyes
to lighten the ravages of the night before.

FULL-FAT MAYONNAISE as a pre-shampoo treatment for parched hair.
(Sounds disgusting, I know, but works a treat to leave dry
tresses silky soft!)

Two Rasam Recipes
Fiery south Indian soup to get those senses going

My dad would argue that nothing beats the common cold, or any ailment for that matter, like a swig of brandy. But I have a three-pronged strategy to blitz the sniffles – echinacea, honey-and-lemon drinks and my most recent discovery, Rasam.

The dish can be little more than water tempered with pungent spices or a light-textured but heady dal. Whatever you go for, the end result is always the same – a steaming hot bowl packed with a powerful punch to get a red-nosed you back on track.

Tomato Rasam

Serves 4
Vegetarian
4 tbsp toor
    (split yellow) lentils
2 medium tomatoes
2.5cm (1in) ball fresh
    tamarind or 1 tbsp
    tamarind paste
2 tbsp coriander seeds
2 tsp cumin seeds
10 dried long red chillies
5–6 black peppercorns
1 tsp oil
1 pinch of asafoetida
1 tsp mustard seeds
2 sprigs of curry leaves,
    fresh or frozen
salt

1. First rinse the lentils under cold, running water, then roughly chop the tomatoes. Place the lentils and tomatoes in a large pan, add 4 tea mugs of water and bring to the boil. Cook for 20 minutes, keeping an eye on the pan to prevent the contents from spilling over (in which case, remove from the heat for a few seconds).

2. Preheat the grill to hot. If you are using the fresh tamarind, soak it in 4 tablespoons of hot water. Now place the coriander, cumin, chillies and peppercorns under the grill. Cook for about 10 seconds and then grind to a powder in a coffee grinder and add a teaspoon to the boiling lentils.

3. The perfect consistency for rasam is watery, with fibres in it. Like orange juice with bits. The tomatoes will almost disappear. When this happens, mix in the strained tamarind water (or tamarind paste)

4. Finally, to make the tadka, pour the oil into a small pan set over a high heat. When the oil is hot, add, in order, the asafoetida, mustard seeds and curry leaves. After a few seconds, when the curry leaves have turned »

a dark shade of green, mix the tadka into the rasam. Add salt to taste and serve immediately.

Pepper Rasam

Serves 4

Vegetarian
5cm (2in) ball of fresh
   tamarind or 2 tbsp
   tamarind paste
6 garlic cloves
4 tsp cumin seeds
4 tsp coarsely ground
   black pepper
1 tsp oil
2 tsp mustard seeds
2 dried long red chillies
2 sprigs of curry leaves,
   fresh or frozen
salt

1. Bring 1.2 litres (2 pints) of water to the boil in a large pan. If you are using the fresh tamarind, soak it in 4 tablespoons of hot water.

2. Peel the garlic and smash these with 2 teaspoons of the cumin seeds and the ground pepper. When the water starts boiling, mix this in along with the strained tamarind water (or tamarind paste). Lower the heat and simmer for 10 minutes.

3. When the time is almost up, make the tadka. Heat the oil in a small pan on a high setting, then add the remaining cumin seeds along with the mustard seeds, chillies and curry leaves. Sizzle for a few seconds, or until the spices turn darker, then mix the tadka into the soup and add salt to taste. Drink it piping hot to let it do its magic.

ABOVE Maacher Chop (page 211)

ABOVE Tomato Rasam (page 202)
ABOVE MIDDLE Masala Chai (page 198)

ABOVE Dahi Bhaat (page 206)

Dahi Bhaat

Cooling curd rice with curry leaves
and mustard seeds

Another firm favourite from south India. I happen to have it from an excellent source in India's Silicon Valley that senior IT executives have been known to fire up portable tabletop mini cookers in their five-star hotel rooms and cook this dish with suitcase spices, and yoghurt and rice delivered by room service.

It's not what springs to my mind as I stagger back to my double suite after too many 'networking' drinks on an overseas business trip. But why not? Curd rice (made with low-fat natural yoghurt) is one of those timeless pick-me-ups – like hot chocolate on a wintry day or iced tea on a blindingly hot one. Fresh, steeped in flavour and idiot-proof to make, it'll mend raging insides in no time at all.

Feeds 2

Vegetarian

1 tsp oil
1 pinch of asafoetida
1½ tsp mustard seeds
2 dried long red chillies
5 sprigs of curry leaves, fresh or frozen
225g (8oz) basmati rice, cooked
250g (9oz) low-fat natural yoghurt
salt

1. In a medium pan, heat the oil on a medium setting. When it is hot, add the asafoetida. As it sizzles up, add the mustard seeds and then the chillies and curry leaves.

2. Fry for just a few seconds and when the curry leaves stop crackling, mix in the rice, adding salt to taste. Set aside for 10 minutes to cool for a bit, and then stir in the yoghurt.

3. Serve cool with a big spoonful of mango pickle.

Tip

If you are poorly or on a diet, choose recipes that don't use onions. Turning onions golden brown uses a fair bit of oil, so leaving them out makes for a naturally lighter meal.

Jeera Chicken
Simple cumin chicken curry for poorly tummies

Jeera chicken is the ultimate remedy for an upset tummy. Even worth getting sick for. I have fond memories of overindulging on the streets of Kolkata, only to be told I was going to be punished with this stupidly simple and yet incredibly tasty chicken curry. Those were the days ...

My version uses yoghurt for its soothing properties and as a quick marinade to tenderise the chicken. I've cooked this when I'm perfectly well, for guests, and I hear it was a firm favourite in my sister's university halls of residence too.

Feeds 2
500g (1lb 2oz) skinless chicken pieces (2 thighs and 2 drumsticks)
4 tbsp natural Greek yoghurt
2 tsp cumin powder
1cm (½in) root ginger
4 garlic cloves
1 tbsp oil
1 tsp cumin seeds
¼ tsp turmeric powder
¼ tsp chilli powder
¼ tsp garam masala
salt

1. Make deep gashes along the sides of the chicken, then place in a medium mixing bowl. Add the yoghurt and cumin powder, stir in the chicken pieces to coat and marinate for 1 hour. Meanwhile, peel the ginger and garlic and finely chop or purée using a hand blender.

2. After an hour, pour the oil into a medium pan and on a high heat and, when hot, add the ginger and garlic and fry for 1 minute. When they start turning brown, add the cumin seeds and the turmeric and chilli powders. The cumin will sizzle up after a few seconds and when it does, add the chicken along with the marinade.

3. Fry for 4–5 minutes on each side and when slightly browned, lower the heat, cover with a lid and simmer for 20–25 minutes until fully cooked, the chicken falling off the bone. Add water only if the chicken starts sticking to the base of the pan. This dish is cooked in the yoghurt and the chicken's own juices.

4. Stir in the garam masala, add salt to taste and serve immediately, piping hot.

NOTHING MAKES ME HAPPIER than half an excuse to throw a party.

My friend announced she was getting married. I couldn't believe my luck. Forget overblown wedding ceremony and dining experience, this called for the most memorable hen night ever. I volunteered immediately to send her off to marital bliss in style.

We were only talking about seven girls on a Saturday night here. How difficult could it be? I fired off an e-mail to the ladies, reserving the date. Then got to search for a venue. A central London bar. With free table reservation. A place that would tolerate a bunch of overexcitable ladies. To be followed by dinner at her favourite Chinese restaurant. And we'd all be home at a sensible hour.

Except that sensible and this friend don't go together. Named after a retired French prostitute in *Zorba the Greek*, she is a cross between domestic goddess and Scary Spice. We first bonded over a bitch fest and pack of Marlboro Lights. Since then, we learnt to cook together. She discovered Anda Raita. And together we set my living room wall alight by blowing candles out with vodka breath.

No. This hen night needed to be spectacular. We needed a stripper. I turned to the little black book of the Cambridge-educated brother-in-law. I was asking the right person, he replied smugly. Turned out he was well acquainted with the former Mr Gay UK. A few quick e-mails and the prize-winning stallion had been persuaded to take his kit off for the ladies in the bar for a nominal fee.

The bar staff had no problem. As long as they could watch the show. This was Soho, after all!

We arrived promptly. The evening started with low-key polite chat and cocktails. By 7pm, we were still dead sober. The friend filled with dread about the events about to unfold. She knew little. Were we going to put her in S&M leather? A Playboy Bunny outfit? Parade her around Old Compton Road with a giant condom on her head? I ordered a trayload of B52s to loosen up the group. Our man was about to arrive.

Bang on time, the manager came in to tell me someone was waiting for me outside. Standing below the neon bar sign was the star attraction, a well-formed, if a tad small, South American model. Shaking with fear like a baby banana leaf stuck in a tropical thunderstorm. With a bag full of his underwear selection tucked under his arm. This guy was more petrified than the bride-to-be. Finally – a reason to strangle that Cambridge boy.

My heart sank as I sent for two vodka shots and chose a red thong. A brief chat about his hometown and love life and our man was ready to take centre stage. The performance went without a hitch. He succeeded in taking off his clothes without floundering for a second. The friend had successfully been embarrassed in front of a room full of strangers. We went off to complete our evening with a quiet dinner.

Except by this time we had more alcohol than blood running through our veins. The ladies were warming up for a long night ahead. The waitresses shot us evil looks as we laughed too loudly, knocked over glasses and spilt food on the crusty burgundy carpet. I quietly prayed for mercy. Fortunately, the decision was made by the second course. We were going to move on to a Brazilian club down the road. A few phone calls and the Cambridge brother-in-law joined us with his colleagues. We danced until the wee hours of the morning, fuelled by more cocktails and shots.

The next day was a write-off. Prostrate on our black leather sofa, I reflected on the ravages of the night before. Did I really need that last caipirinha? Surely I could now admit that B52s and vodka limes don't mix? And that two bars in one night leaves me flat on my face? Hindsight is a truly painful thing.

As I gently lifted the rock that once served me well as a head, I realised two things: 1) I am too old for this and 2) I need some serious TLC to get my body back from the brink. Thankfully, the healing power of Indian food is a scientifically tried-and-tested phenomenon. In my home, that is. If I can be bothered to cook, there are recipes to give blockbuster hangover medicines a run for their money. All passed down the generations back home in India, for when recovery is of the essence.

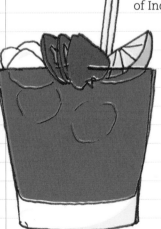

Prawn Pulao
Aromatic rice with prawns –
the perfect mood lifter

It took months to find the right couch for the flat. The black three-seater was perfect to veg on in front of the telly and slowly pass out afterwards. But before I could say 'TV dinner', I upset a bottle of nail-polish remover on the leather, which my man then had to get dyed black again in a workshop in the middle of nowhere.

Didn't stop me from eating curries on it, though. Prawn Pulao is one of those great treat-hangover-on-the-couch meals. It won't spill as I sit lopsided, sinking into the cushions with a vastly depleted brain cell count and a plate of the wonderfully aromatic spiced rice with prawns.

Feeds 4
2 medium onions
2 large tomatoes
2 tbsp ghee
2 tsp ginger and garlic paste
4 cloves
2.5cm (1in) cinnamon stick
½ tsp chilli powder
2 tbsp milk
1 pinch of saffron
350g (12oz) basmati rice
2 fresh green finger chillies
250g (9oz) raw shelled king
  prawns (I use frozen ones)
½ tsp garam masala powder
salt

1. Peel and finely slice the onions and roughly chop the tomatoes. Heat the ghee in a large pan on a high setting and, when it begins to sizzle, add the onions, ginger and garlic paste, cloves and cinnamon. After about 5 minutes, when the onions start to soften and turn translucent, add the tomatoes and chilli powder.

2. Fry this mixture for a further 5 minutes until the raw smell of the spices tones down. In the meantime, warm the milk and soak the saffron in it. Wash the rice and drain it, then tip it into masala mixture and fry for 2 minutes. Add one-and-a-half times as much hot water as rice, lower the heat to medium, cover the pan with a lid and leave to cook.

3. After 10 minutes, when the rice is partially cooked, slit the green finger chillies and add with the prawns and the garam masala. Gently stir with a fork to mix in. Cover with the lid once again and cook for 4–5 minutes until the prawns turn pink and hard and the rice soaks up all the water. Just before you take the rice off the heat, mix in the saffron milk. »

4. Two things you need to remember: don't stir the rice too much or you won't have the fluffy, well-separated grains that characterise pulao; and add the prawns towards the end, so that they are cooked but not overdone. This is one meal you can eat again and again, so make a large pot and keep the pickle handy.

Maacher Chop
Fishcakes with green finger chillies for the morning after

Fagged out from standing for hours on mock-croc heels as thin as pencils one big Saturday night, I could barely lift myself off the bed that Sunday. Forget about bring myself to cook anything. But my Sunday tradition of cooking an Indian meal must be upheld at any cost. So I took the easy option.

Years ago my father gave me a brilliant cookbook by Sanjeev Kapoor, India's first and foremost celebrity chef. I found in it the recipe for traditional Bengali fishcakes known as Maacher Chop, and promptly adapted it. The fishcakes are super easy to make and totally addictive. On a quiet Sunday night in front of the TV, these are just what the doctor ordered.

Serves 2

2 large potatoes
300g (11oz) skinless
  and boneless cod loin
1 large onion
3 tbsp oil
3 fresh green finger chillies
1 handful of fresh
  coriander leaves
3 tbsp white vinegar
1 tsp turmeric powder
½ mug of raisins
1 egg
100g (3½oz) ready-made
  golden breadcrumbs
salt and black pepper

1. Peel and quarter the potatoes, place in a pan of water and boil for 15–20 minutes until soft. Cook the fish according to the packet instructions. Alternatively, I do both on high in the microwave: it takes 10 minutes for the potatoes and about 3 for the fish in my 950W mean machine.

2. When the potatoes and fish are cooked, drain thoroughly and chuck both into a large mixing bowl. Meanwhile, peel and slice the onion and fry over a high heat in 1 tablespoon of the oil for 10 minutes until golden brown. Tip these into the mixing bowl. Next, chop the green finger chillies and coriander leaves, and add to the bowl with the vinegar, turmeric, raisins and seasoning. **》**

3. Use your hand to mash the potatoes and fish, mixing the lovely masala mixture in with it. Taste to make sure there's enough salt. Next, beat the egg in a small bowl and pour the breadcrumbs into another dish.

4. When the fish and potato mixture looks evenly distributed, fashion it into six cylindrical croquettes about 5cm (2in) long and 2.5cm (1in) thick, then dip each into the beaten egg and roll in breadcrumbs. Place the coated croquettes on another plate, ready to fry.

5. Pour the remaining oil into a medium frying pan set over a high heat. When the oil is hot, shallow-fry the little pieces of loveliness, turning them frequently, cooking for 6 minutes until they are golden brown all over. Enjoy with leafy green salad and ketchup spiked with chilli powder.

Mutton Ishtew
Warming light lamb stew with root vegetables

My Indian bones don't do single-digit temperatures. I get a cold from standing in front of the fridge. And the combination of sport and snowing that is skiing is my worst nightmare. Give me a pina colada on a golden sandy beach any day.

This means that snowstorms and blizzards call for special effort all round. Cowgirl-esque flat boots, overflowing woollen coat with matching accessories for the crisp outdoors, and warming one-pot meals to thaw you inside. This light stew is a winner for warmth – a winter staple back in our Kolkata kitchen (where it was cooked using goat meat).

Feeds 4
2 medium onions
1cm (½in) root ginger
3 large carrots
2 small turnips
1 large beetroot
2 tbsp oil
whole spices
  2 bay leaves
  2 brown cardamoms
  2.5cm (1in) cinnamon stick
  4 cloves
2 tbsp plain flour
1 large tomato
750g (1lb 10oz) diced leg
  of lamb
½ tsp freshly ground
  black pepper
1 tbsp butter
salt

1. Peel and roughly chop the onions and ginger, then purée the ginger using a hand blender. Peel and cut the root vegetables into large chunks.

2. Pour the oil into a large pan over a high heat. When the oil is hot, add the whole spices and fry for a couple of seconds. When they start sizzling and releasing their glorious aromas, add the onions and ginger and fry for 5 minutes until translucent. Add the flour and mix well into the onions, frying for a further 5 minutes until the whole mixture turns golden.

3. Chop up the tomato and add to the pan along with the lamb, then cook for 2 minutes, stirring the meat so that it is coated in the masala mixture. Now, chuck in all the vegetables, submerge in enough hot water to cover, place a lid on the pan and cook over a medium heat until the lamb is tender.

4. This should take about 45 minutes. The vegetables will start melting into the light curry. If the ingredients stick to the bottom of the pan, scrape off with a wooden spoon, adding more water if necessary. When the meat is tender when probed with a fork, sprinkle over the pepper, stir in the butter and add salt to taste. Relish scooped up with hot buttered rotis or lightly toasted wholemeal pitta bread.

7.

SWEET INDULGENCES

Irresistible ways to get a sugar high

Miss Masala.

IT WAS BUSY AT WORK.

The week was flying by at breakneck
speed. There were reports to write,
new clients to win over and journalists
to impress. Forget leisurely lunches
and timely escapes; we'd be lucky
to tell the days apart.

Our colleagues in the Marketing
Communication Department stepped
in to help. The consumer girls, as we
call them, are vastly different from us
corporate lot. They look better in little
black dresses. They can get away with
wearing shorts and tights to work, along
with other styles acquired in the Topshop
basement. And they certainly know how
to throw a fabulous party.

The e-mail invite promised an evening of high glamour to celebrate the
launch of a new resort in Mauritius. A vaulted venue in central London was
to be transformed into a tropical paradise, with traditional sega dancers,
lychee Martinis and Mauritian cuisine. Clients and new business prospects
would be in attendance. So would a motley crew of celebs and paparazzi.

Hurrah. We certified PR bunnies now had a celebration to look forward to.
But a party meant preparation. I needed to urgently eliminate the frizzy mop
atop my head. And find something suitably glamorous to wear. Something
told me a shiny suit wouldn't quite make the cut. I took the LBD out of the
wardrobe and tried it on. It was one size too small. Damn. That would mean
no carbs after lunchtime or snacking on M&S triple chocolate cookies for the
next few days.

The loss of sugar was a crisis of sorts for the sweet tooth in me. In my
teenage years, I could go through a kilogram of mithai in one sitting. A habit
guaranteed to win me a hotline to NHS Direct and a lifetime loyalty card for
the Boots dermatology counter if I wasn't careful.

Subtle is not a word that comes to mind when describing Indian desserts.
They are generally drenched in sugar and ghee, topped with varakh (thin

sheets of real silver) and always moreish. Thankfully, having to behave myself for these occasional photographer-filled events prevents my teeth from falling out and my face from bloating to the size of my arse.

As the event drew closer, it got harder to stay off the goodies. I made a batch of Narkel Narus, sweet little bites of coconut and raw cane sugar, and shoved them in the fridge for a post-event treat. Got the dress on all right. With the stilettos. Arrived at the launch after work. Found my way to the cocktail counter. Got mistakenly photographed by ignorant paparazzi. Then made my way home to the platter of lovely little treats. A worthy reward for the extra effort.

INTRODUCING SAFFRON

Reddish-gold threads packaged and sold in tiny boxes, saffron, or Zafraan, is the most expensive spice in the world. Added to Mughlai cooking and desserts, it imparts an intense and rich aroma and deep golden colour to dishes. Just remember, you need only a tiny little pinch to make a big difference.

Kesar Pista Burfis
Saffron milk and pistachio squares

Throughout my entire adult life I've tried, and failed, to bake cakes. Watching the batter collapse into a slim biscuit is probably the singularly most deflating experience I have ever suffered in my kitchen. Second only to accidentally scraping the Teflon coating off a lifetime-guarantee frying pan.

These little pistachio squares are the perfect alternative to teatime cake. You can make them well in advance, arrange them on a platter and leave wrapped in cling film in the fridge until you're ready to serve them. Perfect with cups of Masala Chai (see page 198) and some store-bought samosas.

Makes 16 squares
300ml (½ pint) whole milk
300g (11oz) unsalted
pistachio kernels
½ tsp saffron strands
10 tbsp ghee
1 x 400ml can of
condensed milk

small square cake
or brownie tin

1. Warm the whole milk for 1 minute on high in the microwave or for 1–2 minutes in a small pan on the hob. Remove from the heat, mix in the pistachios and the saffron and leave to soak for 15 minutes.

2. Next, purée the mixture until smooth using a blender or food processor. Now, heat the ghee in a medium pan on a high setting. Mix in the pistachio purée and the condensed milk. Cook for 30 minutes, stirring vigorously and often, until all the liquid evaporates and you get a thick paste that resembles putty.

3. Smooth the paste into the cake or brownie tin, allow to cool to room temperature and transfer to the fridge to chill for at least 2 hours or preferably overnight. Then cut into 16 squidgy, even little squares and serve with crushed pistachios sprinkled on top for decoration.

CAN COOK, WON'T COOK

IT'S NOT EVERY DAY I FEEL A DESPERATE URGE TO FIRE UP A
CAULDRON OF SUGAR SYRUP AND DEEP-FRY LITTLE GOLDEN BALLS AND
BRIGHT ORANGE SWIRLS OF SWEET THINGS. IT'S JUST AS WELL. INDIAN
SWEETS ARE SPECIAL TREATS BEST RESERVED FOR THE ODD WEDDING,
CELEBRATION OR MOMENT OF SERIOUS CRAVING. RENOWNED FOR THEIR
DECADENCE, THEY COME DRIPPING IN PURE SUGAR AND OTHER WICKEDNESS.
OVERINDULGENCE CAN BRING ABOUT ACID INDIGESTION BEFORE
YOU CAN ASK: 'RENNIE OR GAVISCON?'

Indian sweets are within easy reach in those ever-popular
sub-continental neighbourhoods, where I go to get my
kick on occasional lazy Sunday mornings.

ON YOUR NEXT TRIP, LOOK OUT FOR:

LADDOO
Flour and sugar dough ball fashioned with ghee and chopped nuts.

BURFI
Firm sweetened cake made with condensed milk and,
among other things, pistachio and cashew paste.

GULAB JAMUN
Melt-in-the-mouth doughnut served in a warm, rose-scented
sugar syrup. Rasmalai is a creamy version of the same –
a spongy dough ball made with paneer.

JALEBI
Crispy swirl of golden-orange dough deep-fried in a hot sugar
syrup. Divine and devilish served warm with vanilla ice cream.
Try imartis too, the sugar-high-inducing lentil version.

Besan Laddoos
Roasted cardamom and chickpea flour balls

These little ghee-filled balls of gram flour came highly recommended in one of my cookbooks as a great snack for children. By a mother. Now, I'm no expert, but they seem to be the sort of thing you'd give a child only if you wanted them to fly around a room at midnight.

It's my lot to be surrounded by unconventional mums. My own swears like a trooper. My neighbour's grew illegal herbs in Indonesia. And most of my friends' mummies can comfortably drink me under the table. This is what I snack on to rescue my pride the morning after.

Makes 8
10 unsalted pistachio
  kernels
5 whole green cardamoms
100g (3½oz) ghee
150g (5oz) besan
  or gram (chickpea) flour
200g (7oz) granulated sugar

1. Roughly crush the pistachios and cardamoms. I use my coffee grinder, but you could just smash them up using a pestle and mortar.

2. In a small non-stick pan, heat half the ghee on a low setting. When it is warm, add the besan and stir well to mix them together. Keep adding the rest of the ghee, bit by bit, and then stir in the sugar and crushed pistachios and cardamoms.

3. Now stir this mixture well for about 20 minutes until it darkens to a warm shade of toffee; the bitter aftertaste of the raw besan disappears and your kitchen fills with a glorious aroma.

4. Leave the mixture to cool to room temperature. Then fashion little balls out of it and leave to set in the fridge until chilled and hard. Store in an airtight container in the cupboard and enjoy for days. (They keep for up to a week.)

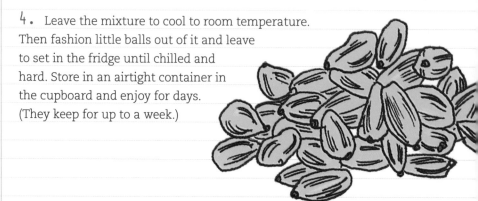

Narkel Narus

Moreish little bites of coconut
and raw cane sugar

A good Bengali would usher in Bengali
New Year with a visit to the temple, a
cultural function, and meeting and
greeting in the community. I do my bit
by collecting all the Bengali girls I know
and planning a big night out in the highest
heels imaginable.

When the guilt kicks in the next day, along with a
raging hangover, I make amends with this celebratory
coconut sweet. Traditionally, it's made with jaggery (gur)
or unrefined palm sugar. But I find dark muscovado to be a splendid
and more readily available substitute. Adjust how much you add,
according to your personal celebratory preference.

Makes 12 balls
1 x 400ml can of
  condensed milk
100g (3½oz) dark
  muscovado sugar
175g (6oz) fresh or frozen
  grated coconut

1. Place the condensed milk, sugar and grated
coconut in a medium pan, set over a medium heat,
and cook for 10 minutes, stirring frequently. Lower
the heat and continue to cook for 20–25 minutes,
still stirring from time to time, until all the liquid
evaporates and you get a sticky, thick mixture.

2. Form little balls out of the mixture with your hands. Place on a plate
and chill in the fridge for 2 hours to set before you devour them.

THE PHONE CALLS STARTED IN SPRING. My ageing uncle and

former local guardian had started his mission to usurp a Saturday night in November for his annual charity dinner and dance. All for the benefit of a new hospital in Kolkata.

After ten years of attending the same fundraiser, I was a little jaded. Inevitably, it was going to be a rainy and miserable day. I would have to traipse down to the venue, in full Indian splendour, ignoring wide-eyed stares on the London Underground. Or blow the annual charity budget with a black cab there. Only to be greeted by the same collection of aunties and uncles, with the dreaded: 'You have grown soooooo big … Remember who I am?'

Worse still, Uncle would drag me around the room. Shoving me in front of his peers with: 'You know who she is?' followed by a headshake and 'the granddaughter/daughter of …' Then I would be seated on a table with nine total strangers and a meagre two bottles of red wine. For a live-music performance, full Indian meal and some late-night Bhangra moves.

I tried my hardest to make my excuses this time. But there was no getting out of it. So I quickly telephoned my sister. If I was going down for the sake of family, she was sinking with me. The husband received an emotionally charged spiel about how important Uncle was to us. And then we all grudgingly gave up our Saturday evening to drive out to the new dinner and dance venue in the middle of nowhere.

The toothy grin on Uncle's face and Indian dessert servings alone would be worth it. Like weddings, platefuls of dessert are the classic way to complete meals at large Indian parties. The usual little sweet burfis and laddoos feature strongly. Alongside more elaborate desserts like Kulfi, or spiced ice cream, firni, flavoured rice cream, and the jaw-achingly lovely, soft, sautéed dessert halwa. Cooked with age-old natural aphrodisiacs like milk, cardamoms, almonds and pistachios, these lavish sweet things never disappoint.

Sis sensibly wore a short kurta top with trousers. But I couldn't let the aunties down. I extracted five metres of thick, south Indian silk from the top wardrobe shelf. Self-mutilated myself forcing lurid burnt-gold bangles down my wrist. And remained outwardly chirpy to egg on the miserable suit-fearing man and sulking sister.

We got there just about on time. The saree was hanging off me like a shoddy toga. As I shuffled through the lobby like a sub-continental geisha, a little girl squealed: 'Look Daddy, a princess!' And everyone turned to look at me. Sis fled the scene. The man ducked to make an urgent business call. I quickly posed for a photograph with the little girl and started moving towards the reception.

The Indian canapés would be running out with every wasted second. I came across a platter of spring rolls. Next salmon blinis. And then came the bombshell. Tonight, people, we are having a three-course traditional British dinner. I choked on my mini fishcake as Uncle delivered the blow. I'd greeted half the aunties. It was too late to run away now.

We sat, bemused, through the melon and Parma ham starter. Chatted with the other diners. Heard all about the progress being made in hospital construction. As the roast lamb main course arrived, it was all a bit too much. The grinning uncle was plotting the family tree of some unsuspecting, long-lost friends. I earnestly pleaded with him. The sis had stacks of reading to do for her esteemed tutors at the London School of Economics. The man had a major advertising campaign to shoot at the crack of dawn the next day. We would need to leave fairly soon to have any chance of making it home before midnight.

By this time, Uncle was satisfied by our appearance and show of support. He was too busy tormenting a new group of acquaintances. He shook his head from side to side, smiling and patting my back. I was being dismissed. At last! We legged it back to central London before any aunties could spot us escaping. Sweet cravings intact. Sunday brunch would feature a ghee-laced Carrot Halwa. The next dinner and dance was a whole year away. This alone called for celebration.

Carrot Halwa
Decadent carrot and ghee-laced dessert

Graters are among my least favourite kitchen gadgets. If anyone knows a clever way to use one without shaving his/her soft hands and fine nails, please contact me urgently. For years, I avoided this recipe like the bubonic plague for fear of the squidgy mess I would end up with if I didn't lovingly grate half a kilo of carrots entirely by hand.

And then I bit the bullet and shredded the stuff in a food processor. The result was fantastic. The texture perfect. And who really cares about the texture when the taste is so good? Roll up your sleeves and don't leave cooking this one for an age.

Feeds 4
10 green cardamoms
500g (1lb 2oz) carrots
3 tbsp ghee
7 tsp light muscovado sugar
200ml (7fl oz) whole milk
1 tsp raisins
1 tbsp cashew nuts

1. Preheat the oven to 190°C (375°C), gas mark 5.

2. Place the cardamoms on a baking tray and bake for about 10 seconds. Allow to cool, then crush in a coffee grinder or using a pestle and mortar.

3. Peel and roughly shred the carrots in a food processor. You will need to do this in 2–3 batches, depending upon the size of your machine, to avoid getting the odd lump of carrot.

4. In a medium pan, heat the ghee on a high setting and, when it is hot, stir in the sugar. As it caramelises, mix in the grated carrots and sauté for 5 minutes until they begin to brown. Next, lower the heat to medium and stir in the milk and ground cardamoms.

5. Now all you have to do is stew the carrots for 15 minutes over a medium heat until all the liquid is absorbed. Stir in the raisins and cashew nuts to finish and serve in little bowls for big impact.

Rose and Vanilla Firni
Fragrant ground-rice pudding

Firni was a staple Eid dessert back in India. After a monstrous meal of meat biryani, bhurani, kebabs and parathas, we would get stuck into a shallow terracotta bowls of this refreshing rice pudding.

The traditional way to do this is to soak basmati rice and then coarsely grind it. I, however, favour the cheat's way of using ready-ground rice flour. The addition of rose water and vanilla is my own twist, but it makes for a very luscious way to end a meal.

Serves 2
1cm (½in) vanilla pod or
  ½ tsp vanilla essence
300ml (½ pint) whole milk
50g (2oz) rice flour
3 tbsp granulated sugar
1 tbsp rose water
2 unsalted pistachio kernels

1. Grind the vanilla pod (if using) in a coffee grinder or with a pestle and mortar. Pour the milk into a small pan, then stir in the rice flour, sugar and ground vanilla pod or vanilla essence.

2. On a very low heat, whisk the mixture viciously until the flour cooks and the mixture thickens to the consistency of Greek yoghurt. This should take no longer than 10 minutes.

3. You need to make sure that there are no lumps in the flour and it is cooked through. If it starts thickening too fast for you to remove any lumps, just take the mixture off the hob for a minute and get stuck in with the back of a wooden spoon to squash any that remain.

4. Finally, stir in the rose water and crush the pistachios using a pestle and mortar. Spread a big dollop on to two saucers, decorate with the crushed pistachios and chill in the fridge until dessert time.

TOP Carrot Halwa (page 224) **ABOVE** Besan Laddoos (page 220)
ABOVE (IN RAMEKINS) Bhapa Doi Cheesecakes (page 231)

TOP Kesar Pista Burfis (page 218)
ABOVE Mango Fool (page 237)

Payesh
Festive rice pudding with cinnamon and raisins

Rice pudding after a meal of rice may seem a little excessive. So this dessert works best on its own as a quick snack before festivities commence. I often make it to treat myself after a week of being good. You could substitute the whole milk for some full-fat lactose-free milk if you are dairy intolerant. It tastes lovely either way.

Payesh is the lighter, less spicy Bengali version of kheer, the north Indian rice pudding. If you add crushed cardamoms, saffron and chopped nuts such as pistachios, cashew nuts and blanched almonds, you'll end up with the richer, more lavish version.

Serves 4
100g (3½oz) quick-cook
  short-grain rice
1 tbsp ghee
600ml (1 pint) whole milk
1 bay leaf
2.5cm (1in) cinnamon
4 tbsp light muscovado
  sugar
1 x 400ml can of
  evaporated milk
1 tbsp raisins

1. Mix the rice with the ghee. In a small pan, bring the milk to a gentle boil with the bay leaf and cinnamon. As it starts bubbling slowly, add the rice, sugar and evaporated milk.

2. Continue to boil gently for 10 minutes until the rice is cooked and the milk thickens. Finally, stir in the raisins and leave to cool.

3. Pour into bowls and chill in the fridge before serving. Payesh is also delicious served warm (reheated in the microwave or in a pan on the hob) alongside parathas.

SUMMER WAS DISAPPOINTING, to put it mildly. Promises of a hot, extended Indian heat wave had failed to materialise. With every chilly evening, the prospect of a short-haul holiday with plenty of booze, food and decent weather became more appealing. It was just as well that a friend had booked a luxury villa in the rolling Tuscan countryside.

Fresh from flying around the world resolving financial crises, our friend, a grumpy Scotsman, assembled a group of well-heeled Londoners for the summer break. Another grumpy Scotsman, his childhood friend, no less, with his American-Filipino banker wife. An indigestion-plagued female IT professional and an Italian-speaking, champagne-scoffing Irish lass. And us.

Gale-force winds and heavy rain lashed outside as we met at the cosy wine bar off Bond Street. There were urgent matters to discuss. The hot-air balloon ride. The day trips to Florence and Sienna. And, most importantly, food shopping and cooking for lazy days at the villa. It was pretty relaxed until the words 'professional' and 'cook' got mentioned in an e-mail trail the following day. About me.

I went into panic mode. I was going to have to cook curry in Tuscany. The expectations were high. What would I do without a cupboard bursting with Indian spices? No kitchen gadgets? Or easy telephone access to mother? My social fate hung in the balance. I packed a large suitcase with white linen, while sipping a glass of Bourgogne. Then threw in the desert island essentials of chilli powder, turmeric powder and asafoetida, mentally reminding myself never to make fun of travelling aunties again.

On arriving there, I ignored the inevitable. First, I flung open the fridge to pour myself some iced tea. Changed into a sea-green sequinned bikini, acquired for a previous long girlie weekend in Cannes. And installed my Indian self on a poolside lounger with factor 50 sunblock. Trying to outdo the tan I last developed during two weeks in Thailand.

If only my nani could see me now, I thought to myself. Destroying the all-white complexion that was highly desired in India and with which I was naturally blessed. Her fears that no one would marry me if my skin tone darkened had largely been unjustified. But she still offered me homemade chickpea flour and cream scrubs to help me return to the ghostly pallor I desperately tried to avoid.

Anyway, she wasn't here now. I baked in the sun like a giant white lizard for four days. Resurrecting only to shower and cool off in the pool. We went through the contents of the starter pack of groceries at lunchtime. While everyone took it in turns to cook their speciality for dinner. Soon, it was my big moment. There was no going back on my word now. I fished out the little bags of spices and made my way to the supermarket. The chances of locating a full range of Indian spices among bags of pasta and legs of cured ham were slim to non-existent. I located fennel seeds, cumin seeds, garlic and a pack labelled 'organic lentils'. So far so good.

But no ginger.

Indian cooking without ginger? This was a serious blow. But I ploughed ahead nonetheless. The man was tasked with chopping and washing, and grinding spices in a muffin tray with the back of a wooden spoon. Friends were banished from the kitchen unless topping up wine glasses. I focused on making Tuscan dal, aubergine raita and pepper chicken curry. We needed rice. Sure enough, there was a large jar supplied in the villa. Of the well-known risotto family.

Curry was served with soggy risotto. This was Italy – no big deal. But in the excitement that was, I forgot dessert. This isn't unusual. In the stress to feed people, dessert often falls by the way in my home. Besides, all too often guests stuff themselves too much with the savouries to do justice to the sweet things that follow. My party favourites are little desserts that can be prepared the day before and served when guests are done with dinner. If they're not hungry, the stash is all ours for later.

We heaped spoonfuls of food on to plates and tucked into the Tuscan curry on the large outdoor dining table. With the balmy summer weather and the Scotsman's 80s playlist for company. Dinner was a big success. Dessert would be served back in London.

Bhapa Doi
Saffron and cardamom cheesecake

Boobie introduced me to this recipe in her east London converted-schoolroom apartment. Piercingly spicy Indian dinner, followed by Bhapa Doi and drunken games of Taboo became a bit of a monthly ritual. I particularly took to the recipe as soon as I learnt each serving had barely six grams of fat.

    After-dinner desserts don't come much better than this. It is so stupendously easy to make that several visitors to my blog post have accused me of having a laugh. I bake little portions in tiny individual ceramic bowls the day before a party and cherish the leftovers for days after. My friend Rosie, author of cookbook *Spooning with Rosie*, even gave it a lovely twist with a topping of Frangelico and chopped hazelnuts.

Feeds 6
4 green cardamoms
10–12 saffron strands
2 tbsp whole milk
500g (1lb 2oz) low-fat
   natural yoghurt
1 x 400ml can of
   condensed milk

six ramekins or a small
ovenproof baking dish

1. Preheat the oven to 190°C (375°C), gas mark 5.

2. Place the cardamoms in a large baking tray and bake for about 10 seconds. Heat the saffron strands and whole milk in the microwave for 10 seconds on medium or for 1–2 minutes in a small pan on the hob, and set aside.

3. In the meantime, lightly beat the yoghurt and condensed milk together until smooth. Crush the roasted cardamoms in a coffee grinder or using a pestle and mortar, and stir them into the yoghurt and condensed milk mixture.

4. Fill the ramekins or baking dish with the mixture. Then place in the baking tray. Fill this tray with enough hot water to come halfway up the sides of the ramekins or dish. Then carefully place the whole lot in the oven for 10 minutes.

5. After this time, spoon a couple of saffron strands and a little bit of the golden milk on top of the yoghurt mix. Return to the oven and keep cooking for a further 5 minutes until the cheesecakes (or cheesecake) have set. A fork inserted should come out clean.

6. Leave to sit for 10 minutes and then refrigerate for later.

Chilli Chocolate Brownies
Soft and squidgy brownies with a spicy twist

The inspiration for these was an Indian picnic feature in *Delicious* magazine. Three ladies, braving freezing British weather, sat in a park surrounded by gorgeous Indian-inspired foods. Style before comfort – I love it!

The magazine's recipe for pistachio and cardamom brownies turned into one of the biggest hits on my blog. I adapted the sinfully gooey base recipe to create brownies with the heavenly combination of chilli and chocolate for real spice lovers. You'll find the cooked brownie mixture is more gooey and less cakey than the traditional brownie batter, and miles better for it!

Makes 16 brownies
225g (8oz) good-quality dark chocolate
150g (5oz) butter, plus extra for greasing
2.5cm (1in) vanilla pod or 1 tsp vanilla extract
2 medium eggs
225g (8oz) caster sugar
1 pinch of salt
100g (3½oz) shelled walnuts
3 medium-hot fresh red chillies
75g (3oz) self-raising flour

small rectangular or square baking dish

1. Preheat the oven to 180°C (350°C), gas mark 4.

2. Break the chocolate into pieces and cut the butter into cubes, then place in a bowl over a medium pan of hot water and allow to simmer on a low heat. Alternatively, place in a large microwave-safe bowl and stick it in on medium heat for 3 minutes. Heat the chocolate and butter until melted but still lumpy.

3. If using a vanilla pod, crush it in a coffee grinder. Add this or the vanilla extract to the bowl of melted chocolate and mix together thoroughly until smooth.

4. Now, lightly beat the eggs and stir them into the chocolate along with the sugar and a pinch of salt. Then chop and crush the walnuts using a pestle and mortar and slit and deseed the red chillies, slicing them finely. Gently fold the flour, walnuts and chillies into the chocolate mixture. »

5. Next, get your baking dish. The original recipe asks for a cake tin lined with parchment paper, but I clearly don't bake enough. I just took some extra butter and rubbed it evenly across the base and sides of the dish. Then I tipped the mixture in and baked the whole lot for 30 minutes.

6. After 30 minutes, take the dish out of the oven, leave to cool and then refrigerate for 2 hours until set. Cut into 16 pieces and enjoy on their own or with vanilla ice cream.

Kulfi

Pistachio and cardamom Indian ice cream

Kulfi is a dense and aromatic Indian ice cream. Traditionally served with sweetened noodles called falooda, this dessert packs a punch on a hot summer day. Just pour it into plastic cups and enjoy when frozen solid.

Once you've mastered the basic recipe, try experimenting with fresh mango purée or saffron and crushed walnuts to make other delicious variations. You could use ice-lolly moulds instead of plastic cups, if you prefer.

Makes 6–12
200g (7oz) unsalted
  pistachio kernels
10 green cardamoms
1 x 400ml can of
  evaporated milk
300ml (½ pint) double cream
6 tbsp golden caster sugar

4 x 20ml (¾fl oz) plastic cups
(the sort you find by an
office water cooler)

1. Set 20 pistachios aside. Smash and deseed the cardamoms, then blend the seeds with the remaining ingredients in a blender or food processor for 2 minutes until the mixture almost doubles in size.

2. Ladle the mixture into the plastic cups and cover the tops with foil. Place the filled cups on a small tray or in a plastic container and freeze for 4 hours until rock solid. If you have a frosty freezer, give the contents of each cup a good stir midway through freezing time.

3. When ready, hold the back of each cup under warm tap water and tip on to a plate, then sprinkle with crushed pistachios to serve.

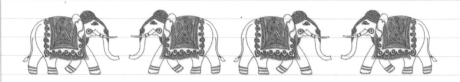

FRIDAY EVENINGS ARE NORMALLY QUIET, REFLECTIVE.

After five consecutive evenings out, I usually need to relocate my karmic centre. My Italian friend persuaded me to try something a little different. And off we went to a south London yoga class together.

I looked around nervously at the 24 Nirvana-seeking faces. Nothing to be afraid of, I reassured myself. I am Indian. Yoga runs in my blood. I lived on a cocktail of headstands and sun salutations until I discovered men and alcohol. Dressed in gym-friendly Spandex, I smiled hello at the linen-wearing crowd, dragged a mat close to my friend and sat down cross-legged.

And then he wafted in. A small, Caucasian sadhu in all white and oversized beads. He turned on Irish-Sanskrit trance meets Hed Kandi chillout and lit some incense. In the background, a basketball player yelled 'f*ck you, motherf*cker'. The unfazed yogic nodded gently and folded his hands together in a namaste.

Is this guy for real? I wondered quietly.

'This class', he stated in a low voice, 'is a meditational, spiritual awakening of the inner consciousness of our self.'

Sorry, what? I glowered at my friend. But she was listening to him with the quiet concentration of the class swot.

'We are going to balance our left brain with our right brain, finally centring ourselves with our highest awareness of our being.'

It sounded complicated. I wanted to go home.

'Balance yourself on one leg, raise your opposite arm and start flapping. Soar until you reach the peak of self-transformation. Unleash your creativity.'

This man's on drugs!

'Higher. Faster.'

I paid to do a chicken impression?

'Now you are going to do a shoulder stand. Stretch your legs to the heavens, then gently extend them sideways and take deep breaths. Feel the flow of power.'

I lay there twisted into an unrecognisable human tower. The blood rushed to my brain. I. Felt. Hot.

When they started singing about peace and love, I finally clocked off and started focusing my inner self on Mango Fool, a healthy dessert of mango and crème fraîche. Some Indian desserts are designed to cool and soothe. Low-fat, fresh and smooth, they are the uncomplicated way to find inner balance.

The flow of power in my home is all about moving from living room to kitchen. Transferring the contents of a deliciously sweet and creamy pot of Mango Fool to the mouth. Knowing it took all of 20 minutes to make. And washing it down with a stiff drink. While quietly sinking into the black couch.

I vowed to stick to what works best next time.

Mango Fool
Cooling puréed mangoes folded into crème fraîche

Have I mentioned I'm not great with chillies? It's not unusual for me to be huffing and puffing over my own curries while my guests look on in bewildered amusement. We chat away through dinner. Smoke gently blowing out of our ears. Eyes watering.

The mango fool is hands down the most powerful antidote to a spicy meal. Normally this dessert is a creamy blend of ice-cold, ripe mango purée and heavy double cream. But I opt for the healthier but equally delicious alternative of lower-fat crème fraîche to return sensation to our mouths.

Feeds 4
2 ripe large mangoes or
  1 x 425g can of
  mango pulp
4 green cardamoms
4 heaped tbsp crème fraîche
light muscovado sugar

1. If using fresh mangoes, slice and peel the mangoes. My preferred way is to slice the top off, then cut lengthwise along the sides of the stone and then slice into quarters and peel. Don't forget the edges of the stone, which often contain a fair amount of juicy pulp too. Keep four tiny slivers of mango aside for decoration.

2. Smash the cardamom seeds with the flat edge of a knife and whiz them in a blender with the mango pieces or canned mango pulp. Check for sugar, adding some if your mangoes are very tart.

3. Finally, mix the mango purée evenly with the crème fraîche and spoon into four dessert bowls. Top off with a small slice of mango to decorate and chill in the fridge until you need to put out the fire.

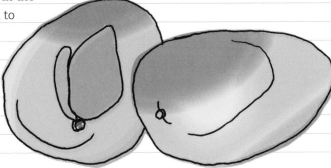

Shrikhand
Soothing flavoured yoghurt

Of course, nothing soothes and comforts like a little pot of chilled yoghurt, flavoured with delicate spices. Shrikhand, or strained yoghurt, is a Maharashtrian speciality from western India. A dessert so light and refreshing that it threatens, dangerously, to make you temporarily forget the spicy fest that you've just enjoyed.

The key to this recipe is to strain the low-fat yoghurt for a thick consistency. Using Greek yoghurt just doesn't work. Then add sugar and the rest of the ingredients, to your taste, and eat ice cold.

Feeds 4
500g (1lb 2oz) low-fat
  natural yoghurt
4 green cardamoms
6–7 saffron strands
2 tbsp soured cream
4 tbsp golden caster sugar
raisins and slivered
  almonds, to decorate

1. Pour the yoghurt into a clean muslin cloth. Tie its end up together into a bundle and hang on the sink tap for about 1 hour to get what we call 'hung curd' – a strained, thick yoghurt.

2. In the meantime, crush the whole cardamoms with the flat side of a knife and powder the seeds in a coffee grinder. Mix the saffron into the sour cream and heat in a microwave for 10 seconds on medium or in a small pan on the hob, then set aside.

3. When the yoghurt is ready, stir in the sugar, cardamom powder and the saffron cream. Spoon into bowls and decorate with the raisins and slivered almonds before chilling in the fridge.

THE LAST WORD

I thought long and hard about something deep and meaningful with which to end this book. I failed. This is a cookbook after all, not a profound piece of literary genius. If anything, I hope it inspires you to believe that Indian cooking is neither an art nor a science. It is merely an excellent way to fill your belly, seal friendships and spoil special people. So you may not get it right the first time. There may be a few burnt onions, charred pots and stained clothes along the way. But it will be worth every minute in the end.

Glossary

Please note that all terms are in Hindi, the official language of India, unless otherwise specified.

achari pickled or cooked with pickling spices

ajwain a sharp-tasting spice used in pickling and for other dishes; also known as carom seeds (see the box on page 56)

aloo potato

amchoor dried mango powder (see the box on page 66)

andaaz approximations

asafoetida dried and powdered gum derived from the sap of a variety of fennel; this is a foul-smelling spice that, once cooked, infuses a dish with a wonderful flavour

atta wholegrain flour used to make rotis/chappatis

baingan aubergine

basmati literally meaning 'fragrant', this long-grain rice is originally from the foothills of the Himalayas and has a distinctive, nutty, aromatic flavour

beguni Bengali aubergine fritters

besan chickpea flour; also known as gram flour

bhaat 'cooked rice' in Bengali

bhaja 'fried' in Bengali

bhaji generic word for dry vegetables, i.e. without curry. Also refers to a crispy, deep-fried flour fritter

bhalo 'good' in Bengali

bhapa 'steamed' in Bengali

bharta mash

bharwan filled or stuffed

bhelpuri a popular street food – puffed rice mixed with sweet chutney and other ingredients (see the box on page 89)

bhodro 'well behaved' in Bengali

bhog/puja bhog cooked food offered to Indian gods during religious ceremonies, which is then eaten by worshippers

bhujia scrambled; the word sometimes also refers to a crispy, deep-fried flour fritter

bhuna/bhuno (*see also kosha*) to fry or sauté spices and meat in their own juices without the addition of water

biryani slow-cooked aromatic rice and meat dish that originated in the Mughal era

bonda croquettes originally from south India

boondi little chickpea flour ball

boti meat, usually goat

bhurani minty savoury yoghurt served alongside biryani in the state of Lucknow

burfi sweet made from condensed milk

chaap meat chop marinated in spices

channa dal split yellow lentils; related to the chickpea (see the box on page 30)

chappati see roti

chenchki 'sautéed' in Bengali

chingri 'prawn' in Bengali

chokro 'boy' in Gujarati

cholar made out of channa (split yellow lentils)

curry literally 'sauce' or 'gravy'; in Britain, it is taken to mean any dish from the Indian sub-continent

dahi yoghurt

dal lentils or the stew made from different types of lentil (see the box on page 30)

desi belonging to our country or 'des'. Also used as Hindi slang for a person of sub-continental Asian origin

dhaniya coriander

dhansak Parsi meat and lentil curry; dhan means 'rice' and saak means 'meat and lentils'

doi 'yoghurt' in Bengali

dosakai/dosakaya cucumber/with cucumber

Durga Puja celebration of the Hindu goddess Durga

Eid or Eid ul-Fitr, holiday marking the end of Ramadan, the Islamic Holy Month of Fasting

ghee clarified butter

gobi cauliflower

golda chingri giant prawns available in Bengal and cooked especially for celebrations

gora/gori Hindi for 'white (male/female)'; not derogatory

gosht meat, most often lamb and sometimes beef, used in curry; in India, it would tend to be goat

gram chickpea flour; also known as besan

hariyali green or greenery

jaldi quickly

jardaloo apricots

jeera cumin

jhalmuri a popular street food – savoury puffed rice mixed with other ingredients (see the box on page 89); jhal means 'spicy' and muri is 'puffed rice' in Bengali

kachumbar finely chopped salad vegetables

kadai heavy-bottomed wok with two handles

kala namak black rock salt with a sharp sulphuric taste that complements certain foods such as yoghurt

kasoori methi dried fenugreek leaves (see the box on page 25)

kathi roll kebab wrapped in a paratha; a type of Indian street food

kebab generic term used to describe meat and other ingredients grilled on a high heat

keema minced meat, usually lamb or beef

kesar saffron

khichdi pronounced 'kich-ree'; lentil and rice dish

khichuri Bengali version of khichdi

kolmi 'prawn' in Parsi

korma creamy curry dish made with yoghurt, nut and seed pastes and, in south India, with coconut milk

kosha (*see also bhuna/bhuno*) to fry or sauté spices and meat in their own juices without the addition of water

kurta loose shirt with deep slits on either side

laddoo sweet dough ball

lassi yoghurt-based drink

lasuni 'garlicky' or 'with garlic'

maach/maacher/maachli different forms of the same word for 'fish'

makhani with butter

malai cream

mangsho mutton (usually goat) in Bengali

masala a dried spice, whole or powdered, or a mixture of spices; it can also be a paste of dried spices with fresh ingredients

masoor dal split red lentils (see the box on page 30)

mattar peas

methi fenugreek

mishti 'small sweet' or 'sweet dish' in Bengali

mithai sweets

moong dal split yellow lentils; green when not split (see the box on page 30)

naan leavened tear-shaped flatbread traditionally cooked in a tandoor

namaste Hindu greeting often accompanied by hands pressed together in front of the chest, fingers pointed upwards

narkel 'coconut' in Bengali

palak spinach

paneer Indian cheese

papad thin crisp made from lentils; popularly known as a 'poppadum'

pani puri stuffed crisps in a tangy sauce

pappu dal in the Andhra Pradesh region

paratha flatbread often served stuffed with other ingredients

patio Parsi-style sweet, sour and hot curry

patra 'leaf' in Parsi

pista pistachio

pudina mint

puja Hindu religious festival

pulao flavoured rice (see the box on pages 170–1)

raita spiced savoury yoghurt served as a side dish

rajma kidney beans

roti round flatbread cooked on a tawa; also known as a chappati

saag spinach

sabzi vegetables or vegetable curry

sadhu holy man or sage

sali 'slim potato fries' in Parsi

salwar kameez traditional Indian outfit of a long top with trousers and a shawl

sambhar vegetable dal enjoyed across south India

samosa triangular shortcrust pastry with a spicy vegetable filling

saree traditional Indian outfit for women, comprising five metres of cloth wrapped over a floor-length skirt (petticoat) and short top (blouse)

seekh skewered

shashlik skewered kebabs

shimla mirch peppers

tandoor clay oven used to cook foods at a very high temperature (400°C/750°F)

tandoori cooked in a tandoor

tadka pronounced 'tur-ka'; spices cooked in hot oil or ghee and added to a dish towards the end of cooking to add flavour

tamatar tomato

tawa flat griddle pan

tikka piece of meat

tikki mini burger of ground meat, vegetables or lentils

toor dal split yellow lentils (see the box on page 30)

vindaloo Goan hot spicy dish traditionally made with pork

zafrani 'with saffron' in Urdu

Index

Acknowledgements

WHERE TO START?

IN NO PARTICULAR ORDER, THIS BOOK MIGHT NEVER HAVE MADE IT IF IT WASN'T FOR:

Andy, my husband, biggest fan and fiercest critic. We did it! **Mother**, who brought me up to believe anything was possible. Even this. **Dad**, a legend in his kitchen, who still finds it astonishing that I can cook. **Doyel**, my little sis, who eats anything I give her. Learn to cook, woman… **Nani**, who resolutely believes I have taken after her and is a treasure chest of recipes. **Hugh Fraser**, my one and only blog master, who got me writing. **Chiki Sarkar**, who confirmed the writing was worth reading and got things going. The team at Janklow & Nesbit. **Jenny McVeigh**, you are the most persistent literary agent ever. **Will Francis**, thank you for wisdom right through to the end. **Jenny Heller** and **Ione Walder** at Collins. Jenny – you have vision and balls! Ione – what would I have done without you? My friends and family who have provided endless moments of chaos and inspiration – mainly **Boobie**, but also **Jon**, my neighbours, especially the **Glengay crew, Lucie, Tanya** and the **Tuscany gang**, particularly **Peter, Gregor** and **Ming. Caroline, Alice, Natasha, Charlotte** and everyone I have ever worked with at The Communication Group plc. You came up with the name of this book, found me media opportunities, read my blog, but still can't cook a curry between you… **Neil Mersh, Joy Skipper** and **Emma Thomas** for making it look so good and **Eleanor Harrison** for finding them all. **Kate Parker**, a copy editor extraordinaire, for her eagle eye despite my protests. **Rob Evans**, who brought the idea of the book alive in his videos. All the wonderful bloggers I have been fortunate enough to meet virtually. **Asha, Sia, Sra, Sandeepa, Indosungod, Srivalli, Jenn, Ann, Elisabeth** to name but a few. Anyone who has ever read my blog and tried my recipes. You made it worth pursuing.

AND FINALLY, I WANT TO NAME A FEW VERY IMPORTANT PEOPLE THAT DESERVE A SPECIAL MENTION:

Leia, my daughter. You weren't conceived when this was. Some day you will value the contribution that gin, stilettos and quality Indian cooking can make to your life. **Dadu**, my Communist grandfather, and the first man in my life. Thank you for a weird, whacky but truly fabulous start to life. **Mum**, my mother in law. You first taught me how to chop a broccoli. I wish you could have read this.

The publishers would also like to thank Dulux.co.uk, Romo.com, Plasti-kote.co.uk
and the Flowers and Plants Association (flowers.org.uk), for providing props for photography.